WOMEN
WHO
inspire

WOMEN
WHO
inspire

A COLLECTION OF INSPIRATIONAL
STORIES TO FUEL YOUR SOUL'S
DEEPEST DESIRES, AUTHENTIC
TRUTH, AND DIVINE PURPOSE

kate butler
B O O K S

First Edition

Copyright © 2017 Kate Butler Books

www.katebutlercoaching.com

All rights reserved.

ISBN: 978-0-9993600-0-2

Library of Congress Control Number: 2017913316
ISBN: 0999360000
Kate Butler Books

This book is dedicated to every woman who has felt "the pull," who has had the deep feeling that there is something more out there, and who is on a journey to explore something bigger than herself. We know you, because we are you. We see you. These pages promise to fill you with wisdom, insights, and inspiration. But, most importantly, these stories will guide you back to the place with all the answers, the inner knowing within you. May you always be inspired to find your way. It is *all* possible.

enjoy the unfolding ...

FOREWORD

What's the passion-fueled project, start-up business or life-style change you want to pursue?

I'm here to tell you, "It's ALL possible."

These were the exact words I spoke to Women Who Inspire's Creator and Founder, Kate Butler, the first time we met. During our first encounter Kate was a new mom and an overworked corporate executive who was stressed and tired. But, she honored her inner knowing that there was something more for her life, which is what brought her to me. During the four magical days we spent together, Kate's zest for life, belief in her dreams and clarity for her greatest vision came back, and came back strong! The most important thing I could have shared with her that day is that all her dreams were possible, and I'm here to say, yours are too.

How do I know this?

I started off as a Secretary and worked my way up to President and CEO of Chicken Soup for the Soul Enterprises. During my time there I was responsible for 230 book titles being published, many of them hitting #1 on the New York Times List for Self-Help and Non Fiction.

As President of Chicken Soup for the Soul, I was responsible for the publishing industry's first billion-dollar brand AKA Chicken Soup for the Soul® in my early 30s. And, I had also created a multi-million dollar training company around the Success Principles, How to Get From Where You are To Where YOU WANT TO BE, along with my business partner of 20 years, Jack Canfield. From his early days as an emerging shy self-esteem expert to becoming a world-renowned public figure and America's #1 Success Coach, I was lucky to be his guiding force—overseeing every deal and watching literally millions of people access the training and insights that Jack had to offer.

As President of Chicken Soup for the Soul Enterprises, Inc., I managed the publication of more than 230 book titles in 49 languages—and became a New York Times bestselling author, producing such blockbuster titles as Chicken Soup for the Christian Soul, Chicken Soup for the Expectant Mother's Soul, Chicken Soup for the Busy Mom's Soul, Chicken Soup for the Working Women's Soul, Chicken Soup for the Sister's Soul, and even Chicken Soup for the Beach Lovers Soul.

As the chief developer, negotiator and strategist of Jack Canfield's career and companies, there really wasn't a project, program, idea, opportunity, marketing plan or career move that I didn't conjure up or know intimately. My career literally started as Secretary and quickly grew to VP of Operations, Finance, Marketing, and eventually to CEO. If I hadn't been there, I am not sure I would even believe it myself. But I was there, and I knew at some point if I could visualize it, and really see it, then I could believe it – And this is when I began to believe, *it was all possible.*

Today, I have the privilege of bringing this experience to individuals through consulting, live events, retreats, women's summits and speaking engagements that teach audiences and groups of all sizes the principles of success and you absolutely have to believe it to see it. But my most important work is helping individuals overcome roadblocks, life circumstances and self-imposed beliefs to confidently move forward and pursue their heart-felt dreams and desires—whether it's a business idea, lifestyle change, charitable activity or some other crazy breakthrough – you can do it.

I believe in you. Together we are better and it is all truly possible. So remember to set your dreams and goals as big as the sky, be patient, consistent, and remember – No is not an option.

Many Blessings,
Patty Aubery

table of contents

INTRODUCTION

A Note from the Creator and Founder of the
Inspired Impact Series,
Kate Butler.

I want to begin by thanking all of the women on the front line of this beautiful movement to ignite more inspiration, change and impact in the world. It is courageous, vulnerable, nerve-wracking, exciting and gutsy to share your intimate stories with the world. The authors in the Inspired Impact Series have authentically shared real stories with the intention of serving the heart of another soul. These books, this collaboration and this movement would not be possible without the brave authors who have fought through their fears for the purpose of helping others by sharing their messages. So thank you, gorgeous authors, you are an inspiration to me.

***

Introduction

It was a dream of mine to create a safe space for ordinary women to share their extraordinary stories. I dreamed of creating a platform for spiritual warriors, champions, survivors, and heroes to share their journeys in a way that could touch the hearts of those who needed it most. These women with these extraordinary stories are dressed up like stay-at-home moms, corporate executives, business coaches, friends, neighbors, and sisters. They are you and they are me. And just as with you and me, once you unwrap the bow that is holding it all together and start peeling back the layers, you find what is beneath the surface: you uncover beauty, you uncover grace, you uncover miracles, and you uncover an undeniable feeling that *we are all connected.*

So grab your book-club friends, your mastermind sisters, or your fellow soccer moms, and curl up with an herbal tea or a chardonnay. You're going to want to get comfy, because you are in for a special treat. These stories will unlock your heart and ignite your soul. These stories will inspire you to learn more about yourself, to start the "thing" that's been waiting, and to take a giant leap in the direction of *your* soul's path. The beautiful thing about inspiration is that it never feels difficult or forced but rather is effortless and graceful. My promise is that this book will not only provide inspiration, but also resources to begin. So I invite you into our journeys. I invite you to be open to the next steps in your journey. And I invite you to enjoy the unfolding.

Women Who Inspire is the second book in the *Inspired Impact Series*. You may consider diving into the first book, *Women Who Ignite*, for more unique stories to inspire, uplift, and ignite your soul.

From our hearts to yours,

the women who inspire

shall we begin?

Throughout my life, I always struggled to find my place. I never quite felt like I completely fit in. I admired people who could comfortably walk into new situations or easily strike up small talk with a complete stranger. In my mind, I was so worried about saying or doing the wrong thing that I would have preferred to just avoid the awkwardness all together.

But as fate would have it, I was blessed with a warrior of a mother. Someone who could command any room, a person who would bend over backwards to help someone else, and a woman who had internal strength that was so powerful you could practically see it shining through.

My mom taught me that the answers were not outside of me, not in any room, in any person, or in any situation; the answers were inside of me. As she guided me through this belief, I learned to look inward for my answers and eventually not only became comfortable in my skin but also *confident*.

My mom taught me resilience, in even the most devastating circumstances.

I think it's natural for everyone to wonder where they came from. For me, this all began with my name. You see, I was named after my mom's sister, who passed away in a car accident two weeks after her wedding at the ripe age of twenty-three. Cathy was my mom's heart. She was her best friend. She was her other half. And then she was gone.

I was born two years later and was given her name. Growing up, I would hear my family speak of Cathy, and the name sounded similar to mine, but it wasn't mine. I would see people gesture and say, "She's so much like her" or "That's exactly what Cathy would have done." But as a child, I did not have scope of the full picture. It was painful for our family to talk about, so it was not discussed often.

When I was about ten years old, I became very curious and went searching for answers. As I scavenged around my childhood basement, I came across a box of letters. One was a note my mom wrote after the accident. In this note she articulated the depths of her relationship with this other soul and the anguish that occurred in the moments, hours, days, weeks, and eventually years after her death.

It was in this moment that I recognized my mom as a true inspirational warrior. Not only had she somehow managed to pick up the pieces and move forward in a positive and productive way, but she was the glue as well, in every possible way.

As I read these letters, I began to understand this Irish Catholic family dynamic and the role my mom played. I started to identify different moments and events and was in awe of the strength, grace, and love my mother chose to lead with. It was in this moment that she truly became my hero. And I knew, if I ever had an opportunity to be as strong as her and somehow show others this power of resilience, love, and grace, then I would show up for this life assignment.

I knew right then and there that this was my path.

And so, ladies (and maybe some gentlemen who may be reading as well), allow me to introduce you to the woman who inspired *me*. The woman who deserves all the credit and all the glory. The woman who is a true inspirational warrior and has been shining the light for my path so I could find my way, without which none of this would exist or have been possible.

The woman who inspired me so I could go on to inspire others and, eventually, create a movement of women inspiring women around the globe.

And, so, here she is: The Woman Who Inspires

Chapter 1

SOMETHING SPECIAL

Some people are lucky enough to have something special or precious in their lives. Some of us are lucky enough to have someone special in our lives. My story includes both.

Family has always been important to me. When asked, most people visualize family as husband or wife and children; my scope is broader. While that is my vision too, mine also includes siblings, their spouses, and their children. This is no simple task, considering I am one of eight children, having five brothers and two sisters. Although my love is strong for every member of my family, for this writing I will narrow it down to one person. That someone special is my sister Catherine, whom I have always called Cathy. Since I was sandwiched between a brother a little over a year older and a brother a little over a year younger, when my sister came along a year later, she was a welcome addition.

My earliest memory of my sister is one morning awakening to find my mother not at home. This was highly unusual. When I asked where my mother was, I was told she was at the hospital having a baby. I was then asked whether I would like a baby sister. My immediate answer was "No!" A few days later, my mother arrived home with Cathy in her arms. I guess my opinion didn't count, because four more siblings would arrive in the coming years!

Even though we had many siblings, Cathy and I shared a close relationship. This was in part owing to our closeness in age—we were three years apart—and the fact that we were both females. Having a sister brought opportunities for "girl things," which we really enjoyed. We shared many things, including toys and a bedroom. As far back as I can remember, we were each other's best friend. We rode the school bus together and played each day. We would play dress-up and pretend to be brides and sometimes cowgirls when playing with our brothers. Our wedding day and what we thought we would do when we grew up were often topics of conversation. As we matured, we shared clothes and makeup. Sharing our daily activities as well as our hopes and dreams often lasted well into the night. During these talks we would offer and take advice to and from each other. Sometimes we gave the other comfort if things had not gone well. We would discuss our worries and successes. Boys, friends, and our social lives were usually on the list of things we talked about. One dream we shared and a topic we often discussed was our picture of our wedding days and of being a bride. When I reflect on all the talks and important events in my young life, I find it hard to think of a time when my sister was not a part of them. My earliest memories all include her.

After graduating from high school, I continued my education by attending college. At this time I still lived at home and worked part time. Our nightly talks continued, and our relationship grew as we shared our daily routines and discussed what was going on in our lives. By the time Cathy finished high school two years later, I was a married lady. Cathy was my maid of honor and helped with many of the preparations for my wedding day. This was an adjustment for both of us since we were not sharing a bedroom or living in the same house, but we still had our daily talks. Cathy continued her education in nursing school and became a labor-and-delivery nurse.

Cathy was thrilled when I told her she was going to be an aunt. We had daily talks during my pregnancy. She would call to check my progress, and we would talk about what had happened that day. We would get together on weekends just to catch up and enjoy each other's company. Since we no longer lived under the same roof, it was our way of staying in touch and keeping up with what was going on in each other's lives.

During my pregnancy, Cathy became engaged and planned her wedding for July. I was happy for her and excited to be part of her wedding. The wedding would take place a few months after my son was born, so she was assured that I would be an attendant in her wedding.

To get ready for her big day, Cathy and I went shopping and chose the bridesmaids' dresses. Our sister Pat and I were the only two attendants, so the selection was easy. With the help of our parents, we also chose the menu and flowers and discussed other details in preparation for her big day.

A beautiful sun rose the morning of July 23. It brought with it the promise of a warm day filled with the joy we were expecting. Later that day my sister would marry her love and our family and friends would gather to celebrate the occasion and wish them well. Since neither Cathy nor her future husband wanted a big wedding, they decided on a church wedding and a reception at my parents' home. After days of preparation, the house was ready, and we began to prepare ourselves for the day. Breakfast was eaten, showers taken, hair styled, and dresses donned. We were ready!

Cathy had chosen a simple yet elegant pure-white dress. Her veil was trimmed in beautiful lace. The contrast with her long dark hair created a stunning result. As my sister walked down the aisle on our father's arm, she looked amazing! I felt such happiness for her! This was her dream come true! The ceremony was personal, and she became a married lady. After we stood in the receiving line at the back of the church, we were off to take pictures and start the reception. Everyone enjoyed a festive evening, and the reception continued well into the night.

A little over two weeks after Cathy's wedding, I received a phone call from my sister, Pat. In that call she told me that a policeman had come to our family home asking for our parents and told Pat that Cathy had been in a car accident. Neither of my parents was home at the time. Communication being what it was, there was no way to contact them. Pat had called me and asked me for advice as to what she should do. My phone call to the hospital let me know that my sister was injured and being admitted. When I got directions to the hospital and called Pat back, my mother answered the phone and told me she was leaving for the hospital. I told her I was leaving too and that I would meet her there. Driving to the hospital was nerve racking; I did not know how badly my sister was injured or any information about the accident. When I arrived at the hospital, I was directed to the emergency room and escorted to a small room at the end of the hall. As soon as I opened the door and saw my mother's face, no words were necessary. Words cannot describe the heartache and pain that I felt that day. I was in a daze. I just couldn't believe that my twenty-three-year-old newlywed sister was dead. We had just celebrated her wedding day.

After leaving the hospital, my family and I gathered at my parents' home. Arrangements had to be made, and discussions ensued. Among the many decisions to be made was what clothes she should be buried in. Would it be her wedding dress or her nurse's cap and uniform? Since the same people who had just attended her wedding three weeks before would return to the same church for her funeral, it was decided that her nurse's cap and uniform would be best.

While at my parents' house that day, I noticed that Cathy's wedding dress was hanging on the back of a bedroom door. Since returning from her honeymoon, Cathy had not yet taken the dress to her new residence. I took the dress home to my house and hung it in a bedroom closet, thinking it would be easier for everyone if it was not in plain sight. This is where it stayed for nearly two years. By this time I was pregnant with my second child. I decided if I was lucky enough to deliver a baby girl, I would name her Catherine after my sister. In July, just short of two years after my sister's passing, I delivered a beautiful baby girl, whom I named Catherine. The joy of having a baby girl was such a healing for my family and me. When it came time for Catherine to be christened, it was decided that the beautiful wedding dress that my sister Cathy had worn would be remade into a christening dress. A friend of my mother's graciously offered to make the dress and matching hat for Catherine.

This dress is so special because it has been worn by most of the females born into our family. My daughter Catherine was the first in the family to wear the dress, and both of her daughters, one whose middle name is Katherine, also wore the dress on their christening day. My sister Cathy's nieces and great-nieces have worn the dress on their christening days as well. When old enough, they are told about their aunt and the special significance of the dress they wore. It makes me smile when I think that something wonderful has come from such a tragedy and that Cathy's memory will live on through this dress. Something special has come from someone so special to me.

Looking back on Cathy's wedding day, I picture a dazzling white dress, soft to the touch, a beautiful bride, and all the happiness of the day, and the vision is bittersweet. It brings back memories of happy moments and devastatingly sad times. This one piece of cloth represents triumph over unbelievable sadness and hope for the future. Life continues, and we all have hard times and challenges we must meet and conquer. Deciding to move on and push forward after the death of a loved one is such a difficult task. Having shared such a close relationship with my sister and having those wonderful memories give me strength. This dress is a symbol of how you can change a situation of much sadness and the memories associated with it into something special.

ABOUT MARY ANNE MUNNING

Mary Anne Munning, MA, earned a bachelor's degree in elementary education, is certified in early childhood education, and has a master's degree in counseling, student personnel services, from Rowan University. She has been an educator and counselor for over thirty years.

During her career she was named Teacher of the Year in two different school districts. She was the recipient of the New Jersey Department of Education's Governor's Teacher Recognition Program Teacher of the Year Award while teaching in Westville, New Jersey. Years later she also received the Teacher of the Year Award from the Pennsauken Board of Education Teacher Recognition Program. Mary Anne served on the New Jersey governor's Core Curriculum Content Standard Committee. She was also named in the publication *Who's Who among America's Teachers*.

Mary Anne has been married for forty-five years to her husband, Phil. Together they have two children and four grandchildren.

She enjoys spending time with her husband, children, grandchildren, and large extended family. She also enjoys time spent with friends, reading, and traveling.

Chapter 2

PURPOSE, NOT POSITION

I am who I am, and that is a person who is driven by purpose, not position. There have been days when I questioned why life's challenges found me so easily. But then I remembered that I am where I am because there are so many who have paved a powerful path for me to follow and allowed me to define my own destiny.

Our experiences make us who we are; our challenges strengthen our resolve to continue and make an impact in the world.

My grandfather, a beautifully colored charcoal man who migrated to New York City from the South, would tell me, "Desi, the most important thing you've got in this world is your name. Protect it and make sure people respect it."

My grandmother repeatedly said, "Honey, you have to be honest with people, even if it burns their ears."

And my great-grandmother used to stand in her living room with her hands on her hips and say, "Huh, bullies never win, chile."

She bought a house as a light-skinned black woman with her own money (she cleaned white people's homes), in a neighborhood that was not welcoming at all—her neighbors tried to physically intimidate and assault her. My great-grandmother never moved out of her house. She stayed defiant. My great-grandmother nearly died in that house and left it for her family.

My mother, a former community activist, raised three girls and taught me to be my own woman and not to succumb to how things have always been done or the power structures that have always existed. My mother was one of the first African American students to be bussed into Bensonhurst, a historically segregated and racially polarized neighborhood in Brooklyn, New York. She was chased from school every day by young, racist white boys who said she didn't belong in that part of town. Staring adversity and bigotry in the face, one day my mother just stopped running. She later graduated from that high school, and of the story, this is what she shared with me:

> You can't let the severely insecure impede progress. The only way to make change is to change how things have been done before. You can't let circumstance and people try to stop you from doing what you need to do. You have to be the change. It won't be easy, and many will try to stop you, but you have to keep going. You have purpose.

PURPOSE

The first to graduate college in my family, I have often been the youngest, brownest person, and often the only female, at a decision-making table in government and politics. It hasn't been easy. But my experiences have made me even more emboldened to live a life driven by purpose, not position.

I almost didn't stay in government and politics. I almost lost my purpose. In July 2003, gunshots and screams echoed throughout the New York City Council Chamber in city hall. I stood frozen, staring at a silver .40-caliber gun that had been used to kill Brooklyn councilman James Davis.

Ten minutes earlier, Davis had introduced me to his associate, Othniel Askew. I found Othniel to be very odd and completely unforgiving when it came to personal space. He lacked it. While he was impeccably dressed, he was also very peculiar. Strange. He moved in very close to me and said of Councilman Davis, "We are going to do great things together, great things. You will see." And I did see.

Before fully committing to politics and government, I had what I called a quarter-life crisis, and it was very real. "What is a quarter-life crisis?" you may ask. Well, I will tell you. It means being young and having too many options to know what to do with. It can be overwhelming. And then finally a life-altering thing happens and helps you determine your interests. I highly recommend a quarter-life crisis because that is how I found myself, my purpose. I was in the legal profession working with corporate clients in antitrust law. One day I was sitting across from a woman who displayed the visible effects of smoking; I was sitting on the client side. She stared deep into the recesses of my soul, and I knew I was sitting on the wrong side of the table. I went home, and I cried so hard that I made myself sick. I called out the next day. I became increasingly interested in the *why*. I wanted to understand what systems were in place to protect this woman, to communicate to her the impact of smoking. I decided I wanted to understand this system called government, regulatory measures, and legislative options. I wanted to study its role and impact and how it can help people. So, I took a chance and gave up a legal career in exchange for one in government and politics.

With stops in Washington, DC, and the mayor's office in Indianapolis, I had finally found my purpose, government and politics. After 9/11, I decided to come home permanently to New York and help rebuild my city. Working in my hometown was very personal for me. Working for Mayor Bloomberg, I had the good fortune of advocating for policies from the Bloomberg administration that benefited all New Yorkers in education, homeland security, social services, public safety, and economic development—things that mattered to me. I also had the opportunity to work closely with councilmembers like James Davis.

But on July 23, 2003, minutes before the city council meeting inside city hall had begun, Davis lay dead on the floor, shot to death at the hands of Othniel Askew.

I stood right there. I was frozen, staring at a silver .40-caliber gun. I lost my voice and thought that this was the darkest day in politics I had ever experienced. I thought I had lost myself.

I was not prepared for that day, nor should I have been. Though some people crumble in the face of adversity, others rise above it. I am one of the latter. Despite personal sadness and anger, that day reinforced my belief in the power of commitment and perseverance and my desire to continue to be driven by purpose and not position.

That experience tried to silence me. But I decided never to allow anything or anyone to dissuade me from my passion and my purpose. Years later I would continue to encounter those who sought to silence me or situations that tested my purpose. Days after the shooting, I could still smell the gunpowder in the chamber and remember Othniel Askew's piercing gaze as he shook my hand. For some, that fatal day at city hall deterred their pursuit in public service and eroded their belief in the political process. For me, that experience strengthened my resolve to become a force to be reckoned with.

When I served as the communications director for then mayor Cory Booker, I struggled to get the media to understand all the hope, progress, and positive things that were happening in a city that was predominately black, a city that was often remembered only in terms of the riots of 1967. I took a chance. We decided to do something that others hadn't done: we decided to become our own content creators. With the support of my boss, even though there were some on our team who were very skeptical and shared it with Mayor Booker, he decided to take the plunge into the world of social media. We committed to highlighting the best that Newark had to offer. I remember Mayor Booker asking me, "Do you think this will work?"

I responded, "Let's take a chance. Let's try it."

I remember sitting in my office with the door closed, my hands on my head, thinking, "What am I doing? I don't even know whether this will work." We took on social media in a time when many in government didn't even believe its purpose.

I took a chance when many doubted the impact we would have with a social media strategy. We changed the paradigm for content creation and development for cities and government. We showcased how a city can take back its narrative. We later ventured at my insistence into the documentary space and participated in a docuseries, entitled *Brick City*, which was later nominated for an Emmy and NAACP Image Award and won a Peabody Award. The idea of fear of the unknown didn't exist anymore for me; I simply wanted to jump in.

NOT POSITION

As the youngest senior official serving in two appointed positions in Mayor Michael Nutter's administration, responsible for redefining the model for big events, public private partnerships, and communications, I relied not on my titles to get things done but on my divine will and focus on moving the needle forward. Every day was no picnic, and the sacrifices on my family were difficult. I can remember getting a call as I was on my way home to put my daughter to bed. It was from my team, letting me know that there had been a bad train derailment and, along with the mayor, I needed to come to the scene. That was Amtrak 188. I called my daughter that night and told her to turn CNN on. I said that Mommy had to work late tonight because something really bad happened but I was safe.

I haven't had a road map or blueprint in this process. I have come to learn that you cannot fear the unknown, nor can you live your life allowing people to try to deter you. We all possess the power within us to define our purpose and, no matter what our role or position, to make an impact.

I have learned over time to trust myself and my judgment. I have sat at tables with President Obama and countless thought leaders, decision makers, and movers and shakers. I've high-fived

Pope Francis, and I have served in various positions in almost every level of government, not paying attention to the titles.

Who I am is defined by my family's roots. I acknowledge that I drink deeply from wells I did not dig. Anytime the road gets tough or people serve to thwart progress from being made or simply try to be impediments in my life, I keep moving forward and, in some cases, right through them, because I know that being driven by purpose and not position uniquely positions me to give the universe all I have and for the universe to respond favorably to the cause in that pursuit.

Being driven by purpose, not position, means that I operate to make an impact in the world and I'm driven by that every day. I don't chase titles, accolades, or roles.

For years, I have been talking about those people who will try to stand in your way, mainly because of their own insecurities, to try to break you. There are those who will try to test your resolve, but they can't crush your spirit, because you are driven by purpose. This is the message I share often with young women and girls of color. I share this message for those ladies of color who may find the trials and tribulations of life and the severe insecurities of others to be overwhelming.

Politics and government is not for everybody. It is definitely a rough-and-tumble sport that can seek to test your resolve, commitment, and will. But everyone can find something that fuels the passion inside of them where they are committed to doing that "thing" for purpose and not position to make a difference. Whatever that thing is, grab hold of it, never let it go, and continue to live a purpose-driven life.

We are living in peculiar times, when sitting on the sidelines just isn't going to cut it anymore. You have a voice; *use it*. Don't let anyone silence you.

My message is my own life story. I have had to work harder, be better, and do more. That's what my mother taught me, because someone is always trying to chase you away. But, as I share with my young ladies all over the world and my lovely daughter, no one can take your power; you are a force to be reckoned with.

ABOUT DESIREE PETERKIN BELL

Desiree Peterkin Bell is a multifaceted communication and political strategist who specializes in building rock-solid brands with global impact. As president and CEO of the public-affairs firm DPBell & Associates, she serves her clients by leveraging her hard-won expertise in problem solving, strategic counseling, and brand development.

Respected for her professionalism and diligence as a leader, she has served for nearly twenty years as a trusted adviser to a dynamic group of American cities and leaders, such as former Philadelphia mayor Michael Nutter, Newark mayor Cory Booker, and New York City mayor Michael Bloomberg. In 2012, she oversaw an extensive communication strategy that positively affected the reelection-campaign efforts for former President Obama in the battleground state of Pennsylvania. Additionally, during the 2016 Democratic National Convention, Desiree served as a senior adviser to the CEO of the DNCC and her team.

A dynamic speaker with a passion for mentoring young women of color, Desiree regularly gives inspiring talks to audiences globally on her life's theme of "Purpose, Not Position." She also lectures in urban communication at the University of Pennsylvania's Annenberg School for Communication and resides on the East Coast, with her husband Brian and daughter Kaelyn.

Website: www.desireepeterkinbell.com
Twitter: @DPBell
Facebook: www.facebook.com/DPBellandAssociates
LinkedIn: www.linkedin.com/in/desireepeterkinbell
Instagram: @desireepeterkinbell

Chapter 3

SURRENDER

Magic. I believe in it. I see it every day in my life, yet it hasn't always been that way. I remember the first time I truly had a glimpse of magic in my life. It didn't seem like magic, and I definitely wouldn't have called it that at the time, but it was the space in between, the portal to creating a whole new existence in my life. It was the breakdown before the breakthrough, the magical moment when all was lost and all was to be gained.

I have revisited that moment several times over the past eight years, and only in the last year did I really understand the meaning of this moment and the catapult it was going to bring into my life. I didn't know about meditation, peace, spirituality, or even self-love at that point. Although I was years past my drug-laden and eating-disorder days, I was still a mess of hijacked emotions and insecurities. I had never dealt with my sexual trauma and abandonment, and one can go on for only so long before one drowns in an ocean of anger, resentment, and fear.

It was the foundation for a magical-carpet ride that will forever change the trajectory of millions of people around the world, because it changed mine. It was Saint Patty's Day 2008, and I was blazingly drunk, crawling the streets of West Palm Beach. I felt as if my life was slipping past me, as I was going through a breakup and losing my home, had just been fired from my job, and that day had found out that the woman I thought I loved was sleeping with our closest friend. I was on a path of destruction, and my first soul guide would come to my rescue.

I awoke the next morning on the couch with a sense of numbness and peace that washed over me for nearly forty-eight hours. I asked my friend what she had done to me, and she just smiled and said, "I took your pain for now." It was my first encounter with another realm, with healers, with soul work. She was the doorway into my creating a life and business that brought others to healing their minds, bodies, and lives and creating businesses from their mess.

My life did not immediately get better; in fact, anytime you decide to partner with the universe and live a life of purpose, things will undoubtedly get far worse before they get better. A few months later, I came home to an eviction notice and three days to evacuate my home of two years. That day, as I quickly packed, I vowed never to experience this again. I spent the next eight months homeless, drifting from couch to couch, sleeping in my car, and discovering who I was in my brokenness.

I slowly surrendered to life and the magic of it and began to take small steps to my healing and recovery. By 2014, I had created my own business and was having my first conference, Pure BodyLove, a two-day retreat that was scheduled the same weekend as Oprah's big two-day event in Miami. I competed to fill my event against someone I held in high esteem.

As I stood on stage in my porcelain-cream dress, staring through thick goggles, demonstrating the breakthrough experience for my audience, I felt a rush of knowing and excitement as I held the two pieces of the once-whole board high above my head that I had just finished smashing in two with my hand. The physical symbol of a mental breakthrough that I had finally had. I stared at the audience below, my tribe that had gathered for this two-day conference, and my heart was filled with pride, joy, and love. The ticking of the hands forcibly coming together as they applauded my breakthrough was like a meditative force, and I was held in awe of what I had created and how lives were transforming in front of my very eyes.

I knew at that moment that the synchronistic events that had landed me as a leader in front of 141 people were by no accident. I felt the first intuitive knowing that my gift lay in this gathering of souls to heal and transform. I understood, although not consciously yet, that this fragment would forever change my trajectory in this lifetime. This was the beginning of something big, something beyond myself; this was the next lesson in surrendering. I had vowed to win, and I was doing all I could to control the sense of terror that still lurked inside.

Flash, and the moment was gone. The event was over. I sat with my small team, my partner, my aunt, and my daughter, calculating the results, my heart and mind reeling in despair as I realized I couldn't pay the bills; we had not made enough money to cover our expenses. I went into a whirlwind, and the fear slowly crept into my life. I felt as if I had flashed back to 2008, my world falling around me. Again I recovered and kept forcibly pushing forward with an iron will and A-type masculine force. It would take another year before my life would completely come to a halt for me to truly listen to the magic that was waiting for me and surrender to divine feminine flow.

The magic that I have experienced is a simple formula to help you live a life of purpose and surrender and allow the universe to guide you instead of you always forcing the situation. Over the past eight years, working with thousands of clients all over the world, I have developed a healing modality that helps them break through trauma and fear, just as I had to for myself. Intuitive Intelligence is a healing method based on quantum physics, neuroscience, psychology, and ancient wisdom traditions that are changing lives around the world. This new healing method is my masterpiece and gift to the world that helps others to transform and heal through all space and time.

We all have a masterpiece in us, a process that is pure *magic* that will bring our purpose to life and create massive and profound change in the world. Here is my simple formula for finding your masterpiece and one that I teach to my clients and take them through step by step to help them create a global impact.

M: Message: We all have a story that lies within us that must be shared. If you want to change lives and heal yours, then you must share your story from a place of empowerment and create a profound message that reaches your tribe.

A: Alignment: When we are in alignment, nothing can stop us from achieving our dreams. We will persist even when the goal feels unobtainable. Your message needs to be in alignment with your core values, and your life needs to be in alignment with your masterpiece. Living or doing out of fear will not create what you desire.

G: Gratitude through trauma: It's not enough to have gratitude for the good. Find gratitude for the trauma, for the pain, and for the lessons. When you are truly grateful for the shit in your life, that is when grace kicks in and magic takes over.

I: Impact: What are you truly passionate about? I have found that when we contribute to the world at large beyond ourselves, it creates huge transformations and shifts in our own lives. Pick a cause, get involved, give back, take your message, and create a global impact that is beyond you.

C: Consecrated process: Create something that is sacred to you. Take your masterpiece and turn it into a sacred process, make it a habit, create rituals, and then share that with others. Better yet, build a business around it, and help the world shift to a new consciousness.

ABOUT MELISSA BINKLEY

Melissa Binkley is a former self-hater who is now a love leader and the CEO and founder of Melissa S. Binkley International and the Intuitive Intelligence Academy. She is an entrepreneur, international transformational speaker, a best-selling author, and world-renowned life and business strategist. Known for her ability to transcend limiting beliefs, she uses several techniques that fuse science, whole-brain learning, personal development, and the quantum field. In 2014, Melissa developed her own mode of spiritual transformational process called Intuitive Intelligence that is changing the way coaches, healers, and speakers connect with their audiences and transform lives through this new healing modality. Melissa is on a mission to raise social, sustainable, conscious awareness and spirituality through a holistic approach to soulistic mentorship through supporting healers, creatives, artists, light workers, highly sensitive coaches, and speakers to live their purpose and tap into Intuitive Intelligence to create a global impact. She believes you can curse, have tattoos, own guns, dance till dawn, and still be spiritual. Exotic countries, yoga, hiking, and green matcha lattes light her up. She intends to raise the vibration of one billion people and heal trauma through her humanitarian work. Melissa is also a guest teacher for the Institute for Integrative Nutrition and is on the Advisory Committee for the Woman's Economic Forum and Board of Directors for I Am

Her Voice. Melissa is passionate about helping victims of sexual trafficking and domestic abuse through her humanitarian travels.

Facebook: https://www.facebook.com/melissasbinkley

https://www.facebook.com/IntuitiveIntelligenceAcademy/

@melissasbinkley

Twitter: @melissasbinkley

Instagram: @melissa.s.binkley

Websites:

http://melissabinkley.com/

http://melissabinkley.com/

http://intuitiveintelligenceacademy.com/

http://intuitiveintelligenceacademy.com/

Chapter 4

IT IS IN GIVING THAT WE RECEIVE

When you are young, you never know where that great love will come from. The unconditional kind. The kind that knows no bounds. The kind that keeps on giving and growing. The love that teaches you everything there is to know about love.

Like most of the crowd, I entered corporate America right out of school. I worked for one of the three largest fleet leasing companies in the world. I was in the auditing department, which I enjoyed because I loved working with numbers. It didn't take long for me to realize that this was a trap! I would be stuck here five days a week with only two weeks off per year unless I escaped corporate America.

After careful consideration, I decided to go to barbering school. I continued my nine-to-five job while going to school evenings and Saturdays. Cutting hair was *fun*! I definitely had a talent for precision hair cutting. I enjoyed my work and I met many great people. But one thing was happening. There is a big limit on income! It's like a glass ceiling because you can only schedule a certain amount of appointments in one day. After that, the only way to get a raise is to increase prices. Not something you can do that often. And let's not forget about the complete exhaustion that hits you every Saturday after standing all week.

After twenty years of this headache, I headed back to school, this time for a medical billing career. I got a job in that field while continuing to cut hair one night a week and every Saturday. In addition, I was taking billing and coding classes two to three nights per week. I was only about a year into this when I opened my own medical billing company with two other women from my office. What a mistake! I felt like I was running an adult day care. *Now What?*

All this time and work and I was miserable. It certainly was not like I thought it would be. I expected to receive some gratification and enjoyment but I was sadly mistaken. Again, I found myself wondering what to do.

You see, I always knew there had to be a better way. I felt it and Lord knows I tried to find it. Then it happened. It was October 2005. I found *it* with an international health & wellness company in direct sales.

My job as a consultant with this company gave me everything I was looking for! I could make my own hours, I didn't have to ask for days off, and the very best part – *no glass ceiling*!

Did I ever think I would be in direct sales or network marketing? *No.* But once I understood how it worked, how you get paid, and what's possible, I decided there was no other place for me.

Plus, I was totally aligned with the philosophy of pure, safe, beneficial products. And the products worked. Now, thanks to this golden opportunity, I don't ever have to return to the nine-to-five grind of corporate America.

It was smooth sailing in the beginning. In my company, there are only four levels of management. I hit the first two within five months of joining. I thought it would always be this easy. Mistake. Now the hard part. The ups and downs of building a team. The quitters. The rejections. The unanswered phone calls. But still, I moved along. The only thing plaguing me was not breaking through that third level of management in my direct sales business. I came close a few times but no cigar. I knew it all centered around *fear*. Fear of failure. Fear of rejection. Fear of success. I am not sure which one it was or maybe it was all three, but *fear* ruled my business. Where did it come from? Why now with the career of my dreams? Why did it have to roar its ugly head? I was never afraid all those other times. I was never afraid of going back to school or doing whatever I had to do to start over. Finding my dream career wasn't such a dream after all.

What is "fear"? *Merriam-Webster's Dictionary* says it's "an unpleasant, often strong emotion caused by anticipation or awareness of danger". Hmmm? Anticipation of what? Awareness of danger where? It's nothing tangible, so why do we make it such a big thing? Why does it paralyze us? Why do we allow it to keep us from living the life of our dreams? Fear is a prison.

Humans are born with only two fears, the fear of falling and the fear of loud noises. If it's something else, we brought it in and we are the ones who continue to allow it. William Wrigley said, "A man's doubts and fears are his worst enemies," and I agree.

Although being out of the nine-to-five grind was the best thing for me, it wasn't for the reasons I initially thought. While I was living the ups and downs of a direct sales business, something much more significant began to happen. I didn't realize it at first, but I had more time to spend with my parents.

This time freedom thing would lead me to my greatest role.

By this time, my dad was in his mid-eighties. He was trim and fit. He still worked his business from home, and as always, he was a very happy and loving man. He was fun, entertaining and giving. We began to hang out together more and more. We ran errands together. We made dinner together. And along with my mother, we enjoyed going out to dinner and Sunday brunches quite often. We spent lots of time on the southern Jersey shore in Cape May and Avalon. Life was good! I had this wonderful connection with my parents that few have. It was because I took the time to be present. I took the time to be truly interested in their lives. And I really enjoyed it! Having conversations with your parents at this age is very different than all those other conversations. You see them as people, not just as Mom & Dad. You see them from a different view point. You actually begin to see the workings of their heart and soul. You begin to understand their thoughts and actions and why they did things a certain way. It gives such insight. Not only to them but to you as well! Yes, you begin to understand more fully their joys and sorrows, and it leads to a better understanding of how you became you! This is *priceless*!

So here we are, the three of us, moving right along, enjoying life, enjoying each other and all our time together and then it happened. It was July 24, 2014, when my father woke up one morning extremely ill. It turned out to be the bronchitis from hell. Two rounds of antibiotics and then a pacemaker on August 8th. His recovery from pacemaker surgery was very slow because the bronchitis was still there. Then a third round of a different antibiotic and finally success. By mid-September, Dad was on the road to recovery. That was two months of pure stress and worry! Of course, now that's all behind us because he always took such great care of himself, and he had such a strong will and determination to live to be one hundred years old.

Little did I know that that was the beginning of the end. It was a slow process. 928 days from July 24, 2014, until Sunday, February 5th, 2017, when he took his last breath at 6:48pm. There were twelve visits to the ER, two pacemakers, two outpatient surgeries, two severe allergic reactions to new medications and several illnesses. Some short. Some long. And some very, very frightening. Every time there was a hospital stay, he got weaker. Yes, he rebounded because of his sheer will and determination but never back to 100 percent. Almost, but not quite. It was a slow, silent erosion. A weakening of the body. That's something we have no control over. No matter how much we eat right, exercise and have a positive mental attitude, as he always did, nature takes its course and toll on the body.

There were 928 days of the highest of highs and the lowest of lows. 928 days filled with such fear and stress and worry. And 928 days filled with such joy and love and connection. By the way, my mother's birthday is 9/28. I don't know what the connection is, but I don't believe in coincidences. Maybe it's because she was always the 'twinkle' in his beautiful blue eyes.

Speaking of my mother, I watched as she selflessly put my father and me first. She took a back seat in life while he needed help.

As she watched the love of her life, the father of her children and her husband of sixty-six years go through all of this, she put her own needs on hold so his needs came first. I have seen her do this throughout my life. Her heart has always been about giving. This is how she receives.

Sickness after sickness and there's that thing again – *fear*. This time it was justified. This time I understood it. Fear of what might happen. Fear of loss. Fear of pain and suffering for someone who means so much to me. But something else was happening too. *Courage*. Yes, that's right. I said 'courage'. I found a voice I didn't know I had. A voice that rose up from the depths of my soul. A voice that had no fear. A voice that was strong. A voice that was brave. A voice that would never back down. A voice that had to speak up for my father.

I chose to take my sadness and turn it into gratitude. Gratitude for another day. Gratitude for another hug, another smile, another conversation, and so on.

It isn't the days of sickness and suffering that I choose to remember. I choose to remember all the other days. The days we laughed. The days we went out to dinner. The days we sat on the bench out front in the warm sunshine. The days we drove to Avalon. All the times we held hands. The cold winter nights when we got under the covers and watched "our shows" together. Those are priceless! You can't go back if you pass these by.

Take those pictures. Study those hands. Make those calls. Burn every image into memory. This isn't a dress rehearsal. You may not get another chance.

Being a caregiver has taught me things about myself. It showed me strength, courage, patience and a voice that I didn't know I possessed. But more importantly, it showed me *love*. You see, I didn't have to take care of my Dad. I *got* to take care of my Dad. It was an honor and a privilege for which I am eternally grateful. And even though my heart broke a little more each day because I knew how this story would end, I got to be his voice when he could no longer speak up for himself. I got to spend those sleepless nights, sitting on the side of his bed, holding his hand, having conversations that will remain in my heart forever. Holding hands in the car as we drove to the beach in Avalon, listening to our favorite Italian singers, Il Volo. Meeting them after their concert was such an awesome experience – one of the highlights of our lives. They immediately fell in love with my Dad and kept calling him Nonno Salvatore. That's grandfather in Italian. And how about those five trips to Italy! Sheer Heaven! But it is our night time ritual that I will miss most of all. The feel of his loving arms around me. *The best hugs ever!* What beautiful memories I carry! The moments we shared holding hands in silence spoke volumes to my heart. I got to be the recipient of all those loving smiles. I got to be his confidant, advocate and constant companion. And through all the pain, suffering and sickness, both physical and emotional, he never ever failed to thank me. No matter how many times I told him no thanks needed - "You did it for me and now it's my turn to do it for you" - he still insisted on thanking me constantly. Because that's my Dad – a beautiful soul with a beautiful, grateful, loving heart.

All those thank-yous remind me of the saying by the Persian poet, Hafiz: "Even after all this time, the sun never says to the earth, 'you owe me'. Look what happens with a love like that. It lights up the whole sky."

Now, because of my father, I fully understand the phrase, "It is in giving, that we receive". Thank you, Dad, for showing me. I am so proud to be his daughter.

My dad passed at home, in his own bed surrounded by those who truly loved him. My mother was sitting on the side of his bed, holding both of his hands in her hands. I had my hands on his shoulders, resting my head next to his head. All of us telling him we love him. When I finally stood up after he passed, I felt something come over me. There was something happening above my head, like a bright light maybe. But I felt it pour into my head and slowly travel down my neck, through my shoulders, arms, chest, torso, into my hips, down my legs and out through my feet. As I stood there, I realized this *thing*, this *light* was pushing out all fear. At that moment, I realized that I would never be afraid again. After all, look what I had just survived! Was this his parting gift to me? I believe so.

I know he didn't want to leave us. Even at ninety-five, he still had hopes and dreams. What an inspiration! After his passing, his cardiologist told us how he admired the fact that my father was always filled with so much courage and hope.

My father had a smile that lit up the whole room. When he smiled at me, I felt it. It made me feel like I was the center of the Universe. Worth all the riches in the world. And he never lost that smile. Although the last twenty days of his life were filled with extreme physical suffering, he chose to smile and suffer in silence.

Where there is great love, there is great pain. You cannot have one extreme without the other. The pain of such a great loss is unbearable at times because I miss him so much. But I am so grateful there is no pain of regret.

There's a new kind of peace in my heart now. The peace that comes from knowing I did all I could. The peace that comes from knowing I always made time. The peace that comes from knowing I carried through with courage. The peace that comes from knowing I put my parents first when they needed me most.

Eventually, the bad days will become a blur and the love that he gave so freely and the smile that made my heart sing will remain. Until I am with him again, he will live on in my heart and the hearts of those who loved him and spent time with him.

For now, it's like learning to live again. Except his time, there is no fear.

ABOUT SHAWN CIOCIOLA

Shawn is the creator of the lifestyle brand, *Facets of Living,* which is a platform to support total wellbeing for everyone. Shawn enjoys a career with an international health and wellness company in direct sales. She also owns and operates a Line Handling company in Baltimore, Maryland, which her father began in 2000. It is an honor for Shawn to carry out his legacy.

Shawn's current passion is a project to support the journey of caregivers who are fully committed to the care of their loved ones. She is in the process of publishing her second book and developing a live event program for caregivers. Her "Facets of Living" approach will showcase her experiences as a caregiver as well as provide guidance to support the mind, body and soul of other caregivers.

For more information on how you can support a caregiver or receive support as a caregiver, please visit www.facetsofliving.com and www.facebook.com/groups/facetsofliving, where you will find more information on programs, live events, as well as, tips and guidance to support you.

Shawn is currently being trained by Jack Canfield, in the Train the Train program to further enhance her skills and, upon graduation, will be a Certified Canfield Trainer.

This chapter is dedicated to the loving memory of her dear father, Sam Ciociola, who is now her angel, guiding light and inspiration on her journey to support other caregivers.

Join her on Facebook: @facetsofliving

Website: www.facetsofliving.com

Chapter 5

FINDING PEACE WITH PAIN

I settled on the edge of the paper-lined table and twisted my hands in my lap. My husband, Ryan, sat in a chair at the corner, and I could feel his unease mixed with mine. It was his first time in a gynecology exam room. It definitely wasn't mine. My eyes moved to the stirrups attached to the end of the table. I'd experienced many painful procedures with my feet in those, my knees out in a vulnerable position. The sight of them made my stomach queasy, more so than it already was.

My abdomen had been pumped full of gas during laparoscopic surgery a couple of weeks prior, and it still lingered in my body. After waking from the anesthesia, in a state of half consciousness, I remembered the word the surgeon said. How could I forget? After struggling with excruciating periods my whole life, I finally had a name for the pain: endometriosis.

As I sat on the cold exam table, with scars from surgery, I waited for the follow-up to that diagnosis. The door swung open, and the surgeon appeared, along with a man and woman in similar medical scrubs. I didn't recognize them. One of the strangers asked me a series of questions from his clipboard before the surgeon stepped up with treatment options: get back on birth-control pills or get pregnant as soon as possible. If I didn't choose either option, then the endometriosis would spread, and things would get worse.

I didn't want to get back on the pill. I'd already taken it for a decade of my life. Now that I was off it, I felt as if I could finally think clearly.

My eyes shifted to Ryan's in the corner. We hadn't even been married a year. While we'd talked about kids, it wasn't exactly the main topic of conversation, especially as I sat bloated and sore on the exam table. To get pregnant, we had to have sex, and that was the last thing on my mind. Sex hadn't happened since weeks before surgery, and the whole thing had been incredibly painful, followed by blood and days of pain in my pelvic region. Not so sexy.

If I could somehow get through that and get pregnant, how was I going to be able to care for a child? I was exhausted. What if pregnancy didn't help and the symptoms came back? The pain that came on the first day of my period was beyond intense, with uterine contractions and constant pressure on my abdomen, which triggered nausea and chills, followed by hot flashes, tears, screams of pain, and prayers for mercy. How would I manage all that with a baby? And what if I couldn't get pregnant? After all, endometriosis is one of the leading causes of infertility.

What if I chose none of the above? I couldn't imagine things getting worse.

These thoughts rang through my mind, but I didn't speak them aloud. Fear filled me up, causing a ripple of goose bumps to take over the surface of my skin. It felt as if the room were closing in. I wanted more than anything to get dressed and run away.

Once I was back in the safety of my home, I retreated to the spot where I'd spent most of my time: my bed. My pillow was wet with tears, and a deep hopelessness dripped black over my heart. I pulled the covers over my head, ready to disappear into the darkness. Yet something pulled me back, a small whisper inside. There had to be another way.

As a natural researcher and forever student, I pulled myself up and took to the Internet in search of another way to address this dreaded endometriosis. While I saw lots of stories of doom and gloom, I also came across positive stories of women who were able to manage the pain through diet. My eyes scanned the long list of foods to eliminate on this diet for endometriosis. I closed the web page with a sigh. There was no way I could follow that. Those foods made up everything I was used to eating.

But what other choice did I have?

A couple of weeks later, I came home from work to the smell of Ryan's cooking. I took a seat at the kitchen table, and he placed a plate of food in front of me. I stared at it for a while before pushing it away.

His brow dropped. "What's wrong?"

"I'm not eating that anymore," I declared.

And just like that, I dumped a majority of foods that I was used to eating every day. That was not an easy task, especially since

I wasn't a cook. Eating became difficult and expanded into outbursts of frustration between Ryan and me. I became the difficult one when it came to food. I was very particular about what I put into my body.

As a result, I started to feel better. I was awakened to the reality of just how much food affected how I felt, both physically and mentally. I felt as if I'd regained some control, and little by little I built awareness of my body and how my choices affected how I felt.

Though I was feeling better with the diet changes, the starts to my periods were still severe, keeping me withered with pain and contractions. In the days to follow those traumatic experiences of pain, I wasn't sure how I was still standing, but somehow I made it through, and I knew if I could make it through that, I could make it through anything.

The pain that came with the start of my period made me miss at least a day of work each month. After yet another absence, my boss approached me as I was curled over in my cubicle with all the color drained from my face. She made a suggestion that had already crossed my mind: "Why don't you get back on the pill?"

When I was on the pill, things were easier in the sense of physical pain, but I couldn't deny its impacts on my mental health. For years I'd struggled with low moods that dipped into suicidal considerations. There were more studies being done connecting hormonal contraception to depression, and I think that was the case for me.

The pill manipulated my pituitary gland, or third eye, which is connected energetically to intuition. When I stopped the pill, my intuition got louder, and the first thing it told me was not to get back on it. I listened to that voice and powered through. I wasn't going back.

Once I got past the initial detox phase of releasing the pill and years of synthetic hormones from my body, I did start to feel better, which inspired me to feel even better. I went exploring into the alternative-health world. I tried many things. I consumed books on health and healing and was drawn to Eastern philosophies and ancient teachings in Ayurveda and traditional Chinese medicine (TCM) because they addressed body, mind, and spirit as a whole. I learned how important it was for me to strengthen my digestion, support my liver, and calm my nervous system.

I started to share my experiences and research on my blog, which I titled *Peace with Endo*. Writing was a release for me. It gave me a way to express myself and pulled in my love for research and sharing new ideas. I was out to find a solution, and I believed I could get better. That belief pulled me through in a world filled with doubts and negative messages. I set out to be a positive voice.

My blog expanded into a community of women from around the world who were struggling with endo too. I wasn't alone. Women started to reach out to me for help, and I could feel the pain in their words and shared stories.

A new purpose stirred inside of me to help pull these ladies out of the darkness, one that I remembered all too well. When the pain ripped through my body and I had thoughts of dipping down into the bathtub to end my physical existence, I remembered that I wasn't alone. The strength of these women was a reflection of me.

My emerging passion led me to a school that changed my life: the Institute for Integrative Nutrition (IIN). My schooling at IIN trained me to become an integrative health coach. During my yearlong training, I took on my first and most important client: myself.

IIN helped expand my definition of health. For so long I'd put strong emphasis on the foods that I ate. This gave me a sense of control over a disease that otherwise felt out of control. IIN helped me to see that while food helped, it wasn't enough.

I took a deeper look into all aspects of my life that fed me on a greater level: things like spirituality, my relationships, career, finances, my home environment, and so on. No amount of kale was going to fix the stress that came from these factors. Making big changes in these areas made a huge difference in how I felt, both physically and mentally.

I knew that stress wasn't going to go away. It's a part of daily life. I couldn't control all of it, but what I could control was how I reacted to it. The practice of meditation taught me this. I started dedicating time to stillness because I wanted to be able to manage the stress so that my body had a better chance of healing itself.

Every morning I challenged myself to sit down and be still. That was easier said than done. I was used to my "go, go, go" lifestyle. Sitting for even five minutes in silence felt like torture. My mind raced with all the things I could have been doing instead or outlined step by step what I was going to do as soon as my time was up.

I stuck with it though, and eventually I started to crave that quiet time with myself. I connected with the power of my breath and learned how to use this to calm things down. This was especially helpful when my body shook with pain.

Meditation helped me to discover the separation of my body, mind, and spirit, as well as the integrated whole that was the true me. I learned to discern my thoughts from the divine-witness part of my being that was always listening. This awareness of my higher self came with the fact that I was never alone and that I was understood on a deeper level. This gave me great comfort.

I took the lessons I gathered from that quiet time in meditation, in awareness of my thoughts and breath, and expanded them into more active meditation practice, as I walked my dogs, played music, or sat down to fill my adult coloring book with shades of my emotions. I felt most calm and in tune within moments of creation. I found peace and joy in small moments that were awakened by pulling my attention back to the present moment.

My meditation practice connected me to an emerging idea of spirituality that I hadn't acknowledged before. I was led to the Eastern philosophy of chakras, which are seven different energy centers that line your spine in which energy, or your life force, flows. Emotions are energy, and they flow through these chakra centers. This energy can get blocked up and start to impact you physically.

I was definitely blocked up. For so long I'd run away or numbed any uncomfortable feelings. I stuffed them all in. I had to unlearn all that. Getting present and in tune with myself allowed me to acknowledge how I was feeling: good or bad. That acknowledgment allowed for the release of any negative emotions. As I learned how to feel again, I learned to tune in to the wise messages of my body. I also connected with my true guiding light: my intuition. I learned to listen to that voice inside.

The underlying belief or fear associated with the second, sacral chakra, which encompasses your reproductive organs, is the fear of losing control. This, in fact, was a leading fear of my life.

Endometriosis made me feel out of control. I couldn't see it. I didn't know whether it was spreading. The only way to know for sure was to literally cut inside and see.

The acknowledgment of this ever-present fear of losing control led me to the most important lesson on my healing journey: *surrender*. I did what I could to support and nourish my body, but ultimately I could not control the outcome of that. I could do only so much.

I had to let go. Instead of always trying to control, I stepped back and allowed. I opened myself up for receiving with intentions each time I sat down to meditate. "I *am* open to receive. I *am* open to receiving guidance. I *am* open to receiving help. I *am* open to receiving love and abundance. Please show me the way."

Once I let go and opened up to receive, the people and information I needed to put finishing touches on my healing journey came to me in synchronicity. With the help of fantastical energy healers, I dug deeper into the energetics of my powerful pelvic space and began to unravel and release old emotions, pain, and sexual trauma that had occurred there—not to mention the medical trauma I'd endured from years of painful procedures in my pelvic space.

The emotional release was extreme, as if I was feeling all the pain from these experiences that I hadn't allowed myself to feel along the way. I physically felt the memories of past traumas that needed to be felt and acknowledged so that they could finally leave me.

As a result, the pain with my periods dropped away. They became mild, as I imagine a *normal* period is for most women. My being open to receiving helped return sex to an act of pleasure and greater soul connection with Ryan, my love and partner in this life with endometriosis and whatever's next.

Once I opened up and allowed help and spiritual guidance to come in, I was directed to a grand path of healing and understanding. No matter how dark things get, no matter how hopeless it seems, you're never alone. There's greater guidance out there, and it's working in your favor. There are miracles happening every day.

You in yourself are a miracle, simply because of your existence. It took me a long time to understand that, living in a body that felt broken, which wasn't well enough to bring a new life into this world.

Ryan and I tried for years to get pregnant with no success, and the process came with a great amount of stress. Turns out it wasn't as easy for me as it was for my friends. After eight long years of trying, I'm a step closer each day to acceptance. I surrender to whatever will be.

I see now that while I haven't been able to create new life, I can still create in other ways. I can still stimulate my natural motherly instinct. Even without the fruit of new life, I embrace the power of creation that's within me, and with that I birth love into this world through my words, through my music, by sharing my voice.

I encourage you to do the same. Express yourself.

Creativity is healing. It's in direct energetic alignment with the power of creation within you, the power of creation that *is* you. Acts of creation grant a direct pathway to your higher self.

The human body is an amazing creation, and it naturally wants to find homeostasis, but it needs the proper nourishment. It needs your love. Self-love is what makes changes stick. It's what pulls you through when you want to quit. It's the whispered reminder in your ear that you deserve to feel better.

I finally have a true semblance of a life with less pain, of one with peace with endo. It's possible for you too. You are a divine creation with the ability to heal. Do you believe it? I'm here to help show you how and to support you along the way.

When you live with pain, it's hard sometimes to explain that to others. It's hard for others to understand. It's helpful to connect with ladies who do. There's power in community of women, especially when it's collected under this pulling desire and intention for peace.

That's what inspired me to create Peace with Endo Connect, an online membership community of endo sisters that provides weekly face-to-face support sessions, group meditations, and continuing education for women who are interested in managing endometriosis with a natural, holistic approach of healing body, mind, and spirit. If this resonates with you, I invite you to join us there. You can learn more at PeacewithEndo.com.

Much love.

ABOUT AUBREE DEIMLER

Aubree Deimler wants to live in a world where others are brave, kind, and in tune with their souls.

She's deeply passionate about wellness and inspiring other women with endometriosis to reconnect to a life filled with love and positive rhythms. That's why she started the Peace with Endo movement.

As an author, speaker, and integrative health coach, she has been featured on *Mind Body Green, Further Food, Integrative Nutrition,* and *A Band of Women.* She also hosts the *Peace with Endo* podcast.

Aubree is the founder of Peace with Endo Connect, an online membership community of endo sisters that provides weekly face-to-face support sessions, group meditations, and continuing education for women who are interested in managing endometriosis with a natural holistic approach of healing body, mind, and spirit.

As a forever student and researcher, Aubree has gathered multiple master's degrees in political science and business administration from the University of Colorado, but her most life-changing studies came from the Institute for Integrative Nutrition (IIN).

When she's not writing, coaching, or learning new things, you can find her outside with her two boxers, coloring, or curled up with a novel.

Her number one best-selling book—*From Pain to Peace with Endo*—hit the shelves in November 2014, and her second book—*Energetics of Endo*—is set for release in 2017.

Learn more about Aubree and her current happenings at PeacewithEndo.com.

Chapter 6

WILL YOU STAND UP?

Growing up in a small, rural town in the middle of the cornfields of Minnesota, I dreamed of being famous. I dreamed of making people laugh on a sitcom, of making them think when I appeared on talk shows, but most of all, I dreamed of being able to go anywhere and be someone with a platform to help make the world a better place.

I was a strong-willed, opinionated child who was essentially a walking statistic. My parents were teenagers who got divorced when I was three. We lived in a trailer home in poverty before my mom married her second husband, who was a mean, abusive drunk—until one day my mom took a stand and we fled.

The small town we fled to offered little solace, and I spent every day plotting and scheming my escape, knowing one day I would make the move to Los Angeles, where I would use my strong-willed, opinionated, pull-yourself-up-by-your-bootstraps mind-set to propel me to the success I had dreamed of all my life.

And so, in my early twenties, I did just that.

The first time I arrived in Los Angeles was the first time I ever felt as if I was home. All my dreams were about to come true, and the energy was indescribable. I was able to quickly get an agent, book my first audition, and get my union card right away (a feat I would later find out was a thing of envy). And then, two years into my journey, it happened: my agent called, and I booked a role on a major TV show. I was going to inherit Buffy's powers on *Buffy the Vampire Slayer*.

What? I couldn't believe it. My dreams really were coming true.

The episode came out, and the series ended with one of the most inspiring and empowering montage sequences I've ever seen, and I was part of it. As they got set to face the biggest, most horrendous evil of all time, Buffy realized that she wouldn't be able to do it alone. As she stood looking out over the war-torn faces of those she had enlisted to help her fight the hardest battle of her life, my character became a slayer.

As she spoke the words "can stand up, will stand up," I rose into frame, blocked a punch from my abuser and took back control. My character was literally standing up for herself. It was a powerful image and an even more powerful message that I was proud to be a part of.

In the show, Buffy sharing her slayer power with all potential slayers was a matter of life and death. If she didn't beat the Big Bad, the world would, in essence, come to an end. The stakes were pretty high, right?

I believe they're just as high now, for each of us, every day. And it's up to us to choose the life we want to live—to be slayers.

When the series finale aired, I held a viewing party. Packed in the little apartment where my now-husband Craig and I lived were thirty of my biggest supporters. We moved the furniture around, and the borrowed big-screen TV was set back in the corner so everyone could see. The crowd was so quiet while watching the episode that you could have heard a pin drop and then uproarious applause when I came on screen and then complete silence. Later, I walked outside to take it all in. I felt strong. I felt powerful. I was in charge of my life, my career, my destiny.

Until one day all that power, joy, strength, and control got knocked right out of me in a single jolt.

***

It was a typical sunny day in Southern California, and I had taken a quick break from my day job to go down to the farmers' market in Santa Monica. The market is set just a couple of blocks from the beach in a bustling area called the Third Street Promenade. Twice a week, the city expands the walking area of the promenade a few extra blocks by closing the streets to vehicles so that the farmers can lay out their goods. It's a wonderful energy as people get to interact with those who farm and make the goods, creating a small sense of rural life in the middle of one of the busiest cities in the United States. I love it because many members of my extended family are farmers, and it brings a sense of peace when I pick up a misshapen vegetable or smell the produce that I know just came from the garden—it smells like Grandma's place.

I had just purchased oranges when I heard screaming. The thing is, it was the Third Street Promenade in Santa Monica; loud noises kind of go with the territory. But this was different, primal, and it made me turn just in time to see people, tents, and food flying through the air. I had enough time to think, "Oh my gosh, it's a tidal wave. But wait, the ocean's on the other side," before the maroon car came flying out from under the tents, heading straight toward me, hitting a table that pinned me to the ground, swerving, and killing the man standing right next to me. That man standing so close to me was one of ten who died, and I was one of over sixty injured.

The horror I experienced that day was unlike anything I could have imagined, and my brain essentially broke. I didn't have a head injury. Instead, I call it a "mental injury." I was diagnosed with posttraumatic stress disorder (PTSD) and was in complete denial. When the doctor told me I had PTSD, I said, "No, I don't. I'm not a soldier." At the time, it was unusual for people outside the military to receive this diagnoses. My being from a culture where you pull yourself up by your bootstraps and get on with life made me feel like such a loser, and my inability to be honest with myself about what I was going through nearly killed me.

It was almost a year after the crash, and I was still suffering daily from debilitating flashbacks that would trigger panic attacks that would cause me to pass out. I couldn't read, I stuttered when I talked, I forgot basic words, I couldn't function, and I thought my life was over. It was as if the crash had completely knocked all the joy from my body, and I was just a shell of who I had been. I wasn't sleeping and had refused medication because I knew all too well what addiction can do. I was terrified that I would become an addict so I kept telling my therapist "No!" when he pleaded with me about how I needed sleep. I knew he was right, but the fear was so profound and I was stubborn. I finally gave in. I filled the prescription, and Craig hid the bottle, because at that point I was so far gone without sleep that I was absolutely out of my mind. And one day I snapped.

I sat on the footstool in my living room with the sun streaming in through the windows and tears streaming down my face. I looked around at a room that was barely recognizable. It looked as if a tornado had gone through it—blankets thrown about, couch cushions turned over, not a single thing left on the shelves, and there I sat, in the middle of all of it.

Reality sunk in. I had just ransacked the entire apartment looking for the bottle of sleeping pills that I was determined to consume, not so that I could take my own life but so that I could get that sweet release of nightmare-free, drug-induced sleep. It was then I admitted that I needed help, and I cried. I sobbed until there were no tears left and my body just shook.

I realized that I could no longer pull myself up by my bootstraps, that I, like Buffy, couldn't fight this Big Bad on my own. I was broken, and the only way I was going to heal was to stand up for myself.

That night, I checked myself into the psychiatric hospital and took a huge stand for my health and my life.

In the psych ward, I was able to get some sleep and begin to gain control over my mind and body again. But the joy—ah, the joy—that would take longer.

I can't explain the feeling of failure and embarrassment I felt when I didn't have the strength to move forward. My spirit was broken, and I needed help just to deal with daily life. It was really overwhelming and frustrating to see that people didn't understand what was happening with me. To not be able to communicate because my brain just wasn't working and then realizing that some thought I was making it up only added to the frustration. In the hospital I learned I had to construct a framework for forgiving them and myself. That helped me to stick to the task at hand, the task of tapping into my inner strength and learning to heal and find my joy again.

I don't think people look at Buffy as weak for asking for all the help she could get to fight the Big Bad, but I also think that this is because we often look at characters like Buffy as those who are saving the world. But what if by fighting our own Big Bads on a daily basis, with the mission to create the lives we really want to live, each of us is individually and collectively saving the world?

Asking for help was the best thing I've ever done for myself. It took a long time for me to heal completely and even longer for me to get into the habit of asking for help—and, full disclosure, I'm still not 100 percent great at it. That strong-willed, opinionated girl didn't disappear altogether. It took me three years before I could work and over seven before I stopped having flashbacks. But I no longer have the mantra "Pull yourself up by your bootstraps," because I know that is just a way of denying where you are. Take it from me—you can't move forward if you don't acknowledge where you are. My new mantra is "Pull yourself up by your bootstraps unless you're struggling with them. Then ask someone to help you pull those bootstraps up."

***

It's interesting to think about how many years it took Buffy to really stop and take control of her life. She spent years being the only slayer, fighting demons and monsters on a daily basis without thought, just reaction. She had all this power within her but never thought about how she could use it to create the life she actually wanted.

I believe we all have that power and that Buffy is a wonderful example of what we do without intention when we're trying to deal with change—when what's inside of us is bigger than what we're used to. We've got so much going on in our lives that when something big happens, we tend to just try to fit it into what's already going on instead of stopping and intentionally working to adjust to this new power.

I had this realization years after the crash when Netflix first started streaming and I decided to binge-watch Buffy. It was one of the most profound experiences for me. I went on an emotional journey with the characters of that show, only to have it culminate in the most empowering montage I've ever seen and then watch as my actual face stared back at me.

That moment hit me like a ton of bricks, and I felt purpose again—purpose that I hadn't felt in years, purpose that had been knocked out of me as that car came flying at me. Purpose. True purpose to get back to creating a platform to empower people and, in some small way, help make the world a better place.

With that purpose, I have been able to do things the little girl in that small town in Minnesota only dreamed of doing.

I produced a movie about survivors with a character who went through what I went through; I've spoken to high-school students about following their dreams; I've even traveled the world to speak and empower others to create the lives they truly want; I've married my best friend in a wedding people are still talking about because it was so much fun; and I've been able to speak to survivors of tragedy and show them that they can overcome whatever life throws at them. I'm really proud to say that I've been able to create the life of my dreams and set it up so that I can be an example to others and show them they can do the same.

And so I will say to you, you can do it too.

I'm not special. My story may be a bit flashier than yours, but if there is something in your life that is making it so you're not the happiest you can be, then it's a big deal. It's time to do what Buffy and I did and identify your Big Bad and go to battle to defeat it. If you need to enlist the help of others, don't let the fear of judgment stop you. Do whatever you need to do to stand up for yourself and create the life you want. The world needs this from you just as much as you do.

Remember, you have a choice.

Will you stand up?

ABOUT JENNA EDWARDS

Jenna Edwards is a speaker and writer on a mission to empower us all to create the lives of our dreams.

Growing up with severe contrast—parents playing in a rock band while living in a small conservative town of two thousand people in rural Minnesota—left Jenna understanding the largeness of the world while feeling trapped by the smallness of her surroundings, until an exchange student came and spoke to her sixth-grade class, changing her life forever. Realizing there are options available to us to change our circumstances, Jenna made the choice then and there that she would get out and see the world and live the life she dreamed of.

And she has.

Jenna has lived in Thailand and Japan, traveled through Europe, and made her dream move to Los Angeles, where she has created an award-winning career in the entertainment industry (even becoming a slayer on *Buffy the Vampire Slayer*).

If you want to learn more about how Jenna is using her story of overcoming circumstances to create the life of her dreams as a way to empower others, please visit www.jennaedwards.life

Chapter 7

TRUST THE SMALL,
STILL VOICE INSIDE

I
t would be many, many years before I'd learn to trust the small, still voice inside my head.

This was the clear voice that would tell me, "Trust that guy. He's a good one." Or "Leave that guy. He's not right for you."

"Quit your six-figure job. Step into the void. You'll figure out what's next."

"Train to become a coach."

"Welcome a child into your family, then another, and then another."

"Raise your prices."

"Move out of New York City."

"Let go of that team member."

"Write your book."

"Release alcohol from your life."

"Name your program 'GLOW.'"

"Homeschool your son."

"Lead a retreat in Costa Rica."

The voice was always so calm, so sure, so spot on. I was not raised around calm or confidence, so I had to develop these skills for myself through a lot of trial and error.

Trauma and anxiety and brokenness marked my childhood. I looked perfect on the outside, but I was a wreck on the inside. My own worst enemy—that was me.

And I had to learn how to master my mind, because it was beating the shit out of me on a regular basis.

I don't know about you, but my mind can be a bit noisy. So much chitter-chatter. So many people, places, and things competing for my attention. Bells and whistles and notifications and e-mails and texts and messages. So many opinions, options, and opportunities (or distractions disguised as opportunities?).

Before I discovered the worlds of yoga and personal development and coaching, I didn't know how to slow my mind down and choose my thoughts. I didn't know that I had these competing energies inside of me called the inner voice and the inner critic.

The inner critic was a lot more powerful back in those days. It was mean and criticizing. A lover of shame and guilt and threats.

My inner voice, on the other hand, was kind, wise, and generous, a giver of unconditional love.

And then I had my big epiphany: I realized that I didn't have to believe the lies from my inner critic that told me, "You're not good enough."

How many decades I spent getting tossed around by that shitty idea that I wasn't smart enough, pretty enough, rich enough, experienced enough, and old enough. And my choices reflected that thinking. I would settle in relationships, my career, my friendships, my health, my finances, and my home.

Yet deep down, I felt as if something better was out there for me. How did I discover this?

I started *slowing down* and *feeling my feelings.*

I stopped numbing through alcohol and drugs and work and shopping and TV—and started seeing the world with *eyes wide open.* This was painful. And liberating.

I have to credit *yoga* for changing my life—and saving my life.

As a twentysomething corporate executive working in New York City, I was burning the candle at both ends *all the fucking time.* Working by day. Partying by night. No time for my *spirit* to grow.

No space. Very little light (my tiny bedroom with my one small window that faced another building a few feet away didn't help!).

I was trapped.

Until I surrendered into my portable paradise: my yoga mat. There I learned that the only person I was competing with was myself. No one in the class cared whether I could do a backbend or handstand or put my leg behind my head. Only me. I wasn't being evaluated or judged.

I was there to experiment and play and relax. I was there to fall down and still love myself in spite of my *mistakes.* It was in those yoga classes that I started hearing that small, still voice inside speaking to me, guiding me, loving me.

The critic was fading to black.

The wise inner voice was more potent and clear. And slowly but surely, I started trusting her instead of doubting her. I started listening, deeply. I started tuning out what everyone else told me I should do and instead doing what I wanted to do.

I started disappointing people. Saying no when I meant no. Saying yes when I was all in (even when I was scared).

I truly started living as if today could be my last (because it could be). It could be yours too. Not to get all morbid on you, but I speak from experience.

My twelve-year-old sister, Julie, died from cancer when I was sixteen. A few months later, my best friend Sonda's brother Mark died suddenly. And two years later, Sonda died suddenly and tragically.

(Sonda and I were supposed to be college roommates at the University of Florida, but she ended up not going away to school, because she was too heartbroken over her brother's death.)

Death and I are old friends. I know it in my bones. Now that I've healed my trauma around these losses, I understand what all that numbing was about: I was sad and scared.

Do you ever feel sad or scared? Anxious? Stuck?

I feel you, girl. What do you do in those moments?

If you are vibing on the energy of much of our world, you probably numb out or avoid your feelings. You might try to overload your life with a whole lotta busy. You move into "go, go, go" mode in your business. You put on a slick veneer and look *perfect*.

Or you default to analysis paralysis. You *don't put your work out there* because you are afraid it's *not* perfect.

But let me tell you: Perfection is overrated. Perfection is a trap. Perfection is the enemy, the voice of the oppressor. Writer Anne Lamott taught me that.

Done is better than perfect.

The small, still voice inside of you is guiding the way to the next level of your expansion. Trust me on this. Trust *her* on this.

I have a hunch that you're reading this because you're hungry for transformation. You're ambitious. You have a gift. And a calling. You're something special.

You're a spiritual healer and a creative. And you're seeking more. More depth with your clients. More consistency in your income. More impact with your tribe. More free time with your family. More adventure. More life.

More, through the pursuit of less. Less clutter. Less drama. Less noise. Less nonessential bullshit that doesn't get you closer to your dreams.

One word for you: "yes." I feel this for you, deeply. Because I've lived it.

That small, still voice inside allowed me to transform.

From burned-out six-figure corporate executive to a yoga teacher making very little money (but I *was* happy!).

From yoga teacher to newbie coach making a bit more money, but not much.

From struggling newbie coach to award-winning coach, author, podcast host, and founder of a spiritual-coach-certification school with the most amazing students.

The coolest part? I've built my business *around* my three young children, my husband, and our desired lifestyle. Full-time work hours? No, thanks. Been there, done that in my twenties. I simply don't have the time or the desire for that anymore.

My husband and I homeschool one of our sons and will be homeschooling our other son next school year. This is a relatively new development for our family that I resisted like crazy at first and then eventually surrendered to.

That wise inner voice helped (as always—when I listen!). It was a massive shift and one that has caused my business to evolve to support my family's evolution.

This massive change in our family dynamic allowed me to realize that I work best working with the best of the best: those absolutely committed to doing whatever it takes to fulfill their assignment in the world.

To attract and serve these superstars, I restructured my business to lead with a Go High approach: high-vibe, high-touch, and high-end.

Evolution is the name of the game.

As Oprah says, "The whole point of being alive is to evolve into the complete person you were intended to be."

Evolution is a mix of *spirit* and *strategy*. Listening and leading. Giving and receiving. This is the most potent blend in the universe.

And the most potent voice? That small, still voice inside of you. Some call it God, Spirit, Source, the Universe, the Divine, the Force. Whatever *you* call it, know this: when you listen, you won't be led astray.

You'll live a life beyond your wildest dreams. You'll climb the highest mountains. You'll help millions. You'll earn millions. You'll be all you were created to be.

Dear reader, I'm pulling for you. Time to *get gutsy*.

Ready?

ABOUT JENNY FENIG

Jenny Fenig, creator of the Get Gutsy movement, is a mentor to coaches, healers, and creatives building powerhouse businesses through a potent blend of spirit and strategy.

The sacred mission of Jenny's programs, best-selling book, podcast, and coach-certification school is how to touch more lives with your message and cash in on your calling.

After a successful corporate career in New York City, Jenny quit her six-figure job to do what she was put on this planet to do: coach gutsy leaders to rise to their next level.

Jenny is the founder of Get Gutsy Coach Training School, which empowers spiritual coaches to make a difference and a great living.

She lives in Massachusetts with her husband and three children who make the journey sweet and a little wild.

Jenny is a 2016 Silver Stevie Award winner for Coach of the Year.

Visit Jenny at JennyFenig.com.

For a free copy of Jenny's tip sheet, "8 Keys to Finding + Living Your Soul's Calling (Even If You're Totally Lost and Don't Know Where to Start!)," visitJennyFenig.com/calling.

Chapter 8

THE TENACIOUS ART OF LIVING

Uncontrollable yelling and screaming and the sound of toys being hurled across the room in an explosive fit of rage were coming from Brendan's bedroom. I couldn't calm him down. I tried. Auntie Shell called, heard what was going on, and tried to calm Brendan by phone. I handed him the phone; they talked. It wasn't working; he tossed the phone back to me. As I walked out of his room still holding the phone, Auntie Shell shared what she'd said to Brendan. Meanwhile, he had picked up where he left off with his unexplainable anger. Then suddenly, it was silent in his room. *Silent.* That couldn't be good. I hung up the phone without warning and rushed into his room, and there he was—he had hanged himself in his closet. It all happened so quickly, but luckily, I was quick too. Quick to get in there. Quick to get him down. The physical struggle continued. We ended up back in the ER, once again, waiting for the crisis worker to come. Admittance into the children's inpatient psychiatric program, once again.

How in the hell did we end up here? Not here in the hospital—*here*! This is not how it's *supposed* to be! Day by day, minute by minute, not knowing what was going to happen next. Always walking on eggshells. Was it because as a baby he had a fever of over 105 degrees and was rushed to the ER with convulsions? The doctors had to pack him in ice towels to get the fever down. Or was it *me*? It's *always* the parents' fault, isn't it? When the child doesn't listen or is out of control, "It must be the parents' fault, *because if that was my kid...*" Yes, that judgment. Rewind: First grade. We were at a doctor's appointment with our family doctor. Without me questioning, the doctor told me he thought Brendan had ADHD. Of course this was easy for the doctor to recognize; he assured me that his stepson also had ADHD, and he had had great success treating him with Ritalin.

YOU DON'T KNOW WHAT YOU DON'T KNOW UNTIL IT'S IMPORTANT FOR YOU TO KNOW IT

I just did not know. *I didn't know.* I had faith in our doctor. Surely he *must* know what he's talking about! He gave me a few questionnaires, one for me and one for the school to fill out, along with a prescription for Ritalin. Once the doctor had the questionnaires back and calculated the scores, he would determine if we needed to fill the prescription. Sure enough, based on the answers to the questionnaire, my son was diagnosed with ADHD. He was a busy kid. He loved to talk in class. He loved to get up when it wasn't break time;

he was easily distracted and disruptive. The prescription was filled. Eventually my son was taking Ritalin three times a day. Months later, it seemed that the Ritalin was ineffective. The school completed a psychological evaluation. Before completing the evaluation in full, the school psychologist determined in less than one art class that my son had ADHD and was learning disabled because after coming back from the bathroom, he was again distracted. Later came testing, *after* she had already made her diagnosis based on her twenty-minute observation. My son was on Ritalin at the time of the evaluation. The psychologist never asked whether he was on medication at the time; she assumed he wasn't. Of course I didn't question the experts. I didn't know any better.

Over the years the medication names changed; the cycle continued and even progressed. Our doctor moved out of state. We now had another doctor. I work in the medical field and knew this pediatrician well. He was an excellent doctor. Next diagnosis: depression, and Prozac was added. This is when it got real ugly. Not only did *I not know about the risks involved with this medication*, but I don't think this doctor knew either. As time passed, Brendan's symptoms and behaviors escalated, we found ourselves continually in and out of the children's inpatient psychiatric program. By now he was on three medications. Ritalin was removed; we kept the Prozac and added Depakote and Adderall. I discovered the hard way that often when symptoms persist or become worse, more medications are added. The same holds true with adults. What I didn't realize is that certain *behaviors* can be a side effect of the medication. I previously equated side effects with rash, headache, dizziness, nausea, and the like. Agitation, anger, violence, and depression never crossed my mind. After sharing my concerns with my cousin, who works in the mental-health field with troubled kids, she was appalled that he was on these meds, especially the Prozac. She told me that his behaviors could be side effects caused by the medication and that Prozac was not recommended for children due to guess what: *suicidal ideation*.

BECOMING COLOMBO, CAPTAIN OBVIOUS, AND DR. LAUREN

I called the pediatrician and asked whether what my cousin told me was true. His answer, folks? Yes, he knew the warnings and potential side effects. My son experienced all the negative effects of this drug and none of the positive.

During the case-review meeting at the facility, I demanded the Prozac be removed. I was no longer allowing it. The psychologist tried to persuade me. "Prozac has a bad rap, but it's a great medication."

I saw red rats. I locked eyes with her and sternly said, "Well then, why do we continue to have Brendan on a medication that is not helping him? If it's not helping him, remove it!" He was weaned off.

I am now *aware*, so much so that my family and friends have given me nicknames. I am persistent, I am tenacious, I do my homework, I cross my t's, and I dot my i's. I have an unapologetic fierceness. If there is something to know or find, I will find it; I will know it, and when the time is right, I will show it. I didn't know then, but I sure as hell know now.

GOING ON WHEN YOU HAVEN'T GOT THE STRENGTH

Most days I honestly didn't know how I was going to make it to the next day. No one truly knew the amount of pain and anguish I carried. I would smile for the camera only to lie behind the lens. My family and friends were supportive, yet I never showed how truly broken I was. I worked full time and had my younger son, Mitchell, to raise; I had to persevere. I didn't give myself any other option. I was involved in every aspect of my son Brendan's treatment plan, every aspect of his life. I was there and I was armed—armed with knowledge while continuing to find the solution.

If you have a child who is out of control or who has needs that are different from those of other children, it's common to feel shame, guilt, anger, and hopelessness.

So how did I survive beyond merely existing? Perhaps it's because I'm a Gemini, or perhaps it's because I'm tenacious like my mother. Either way, there were some essential factors that played a role: mindsets. *I decided.* I decided that I would do the best I could and I would not give up. I can't control the outcome or be accountable for the choices of others, not even my own child. I can merely do the best I can each and every day, as we all have the freedom to choose. You'll learn the difference between empowering and enabling, most assuredly the hard way. Tough love is by far the most difficult yet most necessary life lesson for your child. Your heart may shatter into a million pieces along the way. Progress, not perfection. *Perfection is a pressure we put on ourselves with unrealistic expectations.*

Support was an essential element to surviving. Having a support system—family, friends, therapists—was invaluable. They gave me *courage.* Going on when you haven't got the strength means courage. I didn't always find the answers, but I knew that I was never alone.

Celebrating the positives and the victories rather than just focusing on the negative behavior is vital to progress. I assure you: positives exist. I looked for them and wrote them down. It's easy to miss them with so much turmoil swirling about, but I didn't want to get swept away in a sea of negative patterns and promotions. I admit there were failures. Painful as they could be, that's life. But even though I wasn't perfect and failed, I knew that at least I would fail while daring greatly.

THERE IS NO GREATER GIFT THAN THE GIFT OF LOVE, WHICH IS A PRICELESS TREASURE

Fast-forward to Christmas season 2016. I met a lady while at the car wash who insisted I looked familiar. She wasn't familiar to me, not her face, not her name. I asked where she worked. That wasn't familiar either. I asked her where she previously worked. She said she had worked at the children's psychiatric inpatient program. *Bingo!* I told her my son's name. She remembered him from seventeen years before with specific detail. She remembered me. She said she remembered me because I was "one of the few parents who actually cared about their children." As I drove away, the tears came. She had no idea the gift she had just given me.

Today, Brendan is twenty-seven years old. He is self-sufficient and driven and has a passion to inspire others through his experiences. We have a close relationship. We made it.

ABOUT LAUREN FISHER

She was one who never looked back. Was it her lack of empathy or her intense drive? It didn't matter; she forged ahead. She didn't realize all that she had accomplished. She hadn't noticed. To get to here, you start from there. From almost losing her hand in a freak work accident right after high school, single parenting, dealing with the state juvenile detention system, where she spearheaded a regulation change for the betterment of all children, to participating in a 2014 Guinness Book of World Records event, she has overcome and achieved much due to her tenacious nature. Lauren Fisher has held starring roles as daughter, sister, mother, friend, confidante, advocate, Captain Obvious, and private investigator extraordinaire (as coined by her family and friends). She's advanced in her career with a national health-care organization as a corporate trainer, where she is continually inspired by all she meets while striving to inspire others with her experiences.

She has encountered countless inspirations in the twists and turns along her path. She stopped, turned around, and finally took notice. She acknowledged her accomplishments while embracing her strengths and weaknesses. She owned it all, all that she had manifested—the good, the bad, the ugly, the beautiful! Since then, she's been strategically creating on purpose as a mind-set strategist. Since then, she's been strategically creating on purpose as a certified Ignitor Coach™ and mind-set strategist.

Visit Lauren at ManifestinMotion.com.

Chapter 9

LOVE YOUR SOULSELF

It was two o'clock in the morning as I quickly walked down the dimly lit hallway, Kleenex in one hand and pager in the other. I had five-and-a-half hours left in my twelve-hour night shift as a respiratory therapist, and I wasn't sure how I was going to get through it.

That particular night was much like any normal night workwise, but emotionally it was much different. I routinely cared for children who required breathing treatments for their breathing difficulties. Additionally, my duties that night entailed caring for children on life support in the pediatric intensive-care unit.

Here I was, literally breathing life into these very sick children and, at that very moment, in need of life support for my soul.

In the midst of a divorce, I found myself unable to breathe from the weight of fear, uncertainty, and despair.

Something was calling me to walk down that dimly lit hallway to escape for a brief moment in the chapel. I found myself alone and on my knees, praying for direction, for something to pull me out of this deep, dark place, for answers, for solutions.

Feeling unable to call anyone in the middle of the night, I knew I needed to find a solution within myself. Then it came to me. If I could change my thoughts, maybe I could change the direction of my life. I took a piece of paper out of the pocket of my scrubs and started writing down positive statements to make me feel supported and uplifted—affirmations.

Each day after that, I created affirmations that breathed hope into my situation, into my soul. I wrote them out, I read them aloud, and I repeated them. I even renamed them "soulfirmations"—affirmations for your soul. I began to share my soulfirmations on Facebook and created an e-book to provide these words to assist others. I am sharing the most impactful affirmations at that time with you below.

- I trust all that I need will be provided for me.
- I feel supported.
- I release all fear.
- One step at a time, I allow myself to heal from the past.
- I am confident in asking others for help.
- Today I love myself and I move forward.
- I love and I am loved.
- I embrace myself just the way I am.
- I recognize all the love and joy around me.
- I grow from each experience I am given.
- My voice is heard.
- I release the past by finding the love within it.
- I let my joy shine through.
- I move forward in faith and create a joyful life.

Slowly, I began to feel better, yet it wasn't enough.

The affirmations began to empower me to begin to love myself again, but there was a desire for more.

My next step was the realization that as a natural caregiver, I needed less health care and more self-care. I was working very hard caring for others, personally as well as professionally, but I had forgotten to care for myself in the process.

I needed a new relationship with myself. I wanted to reestablish that connection with my deepest self. Coming from a previous place of uncertainty, I knew I wanted something simple and effective. I knew that when I started my mornings off right, my day flowed so wonderfully. I wondered how I could care for myself in the mornings that would restore my body, mind, and spirit and create an act of self-love.

Through trial and error, I created a morning routine that worked for me. I began to take time for myself.

Each morning when I awoke, I would lie in bed for ten extra minutes. I would grab my journal and write out my affirmations or intentions for the day. I visualized how my day would look and feel.

Next, I made myself a cup of hot green tea and crawled back into bed. At this time I would listen to a guided meditation that lasted no more than ten minutes. I even learned how to create my own guided meditations, which I now share with the world.

My focus was not to rush myself but to pamper myself with the gift of time. Through this devoted time for myself, the inspiration came to create a card deck with an intention word, an affirmation, and an action.

This deck of thirty-one cards provides an inspiring and focused way to start your day by drawing a card for guidance.

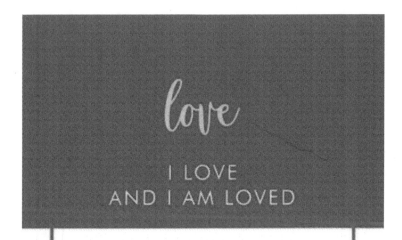

love

I LOVE
AND I AM LOVED

Write a love letter to
yourself or a loved one.
Seal it with a kiss
and send it off.

worthy

I AM WORTHY

Treat yourself today with
loving compliments
and a desired purchase.

shift

I SHIFT MY THOUGHTS WITH EASE

When fear creeps in,
re-frame your thoughts
to the positive.

Once I began developing this relationship with myself, I began to recognize that I was worthy—worthy of more than I was doing or had been allowing of myself. I had overcome the fear, the uncertainty, and the despair. This led me to a deeper level of knowing that I was meant for more. Once the self-love began to align, I was shining bright, and I desired to share how I had pulled myself out of a dark place and into a place where my soul was connected to the divine.

Once I started sharing how I came through this transformation, I was able to teach other women step by step how they could fully immerse themselves into the work they wanted to launch into the world. I knew I was on the right path when one of the women I was helping, who had no income for six months and relied on others for everything from housing to food, booked a $1,500 client within two sessions of working with me. She stepped back into her own self-worth! She loved herself enough to charge for her services.

I am now very clear that my mission in life is to have known the depth of despair to the extent that I was forced to breathe life back into my soul to find the solutions within myself. I now have a foundation rooted in self-love, loving my soulself, which paves the way for guiding others.

ABOUT KIMBERLY FLATLAND

Kimberly Flatland is a life coach, speaker, and mind-set momma on a mission to create a movement. A movement to Love Your SoulSelf. Kimberly has guided hundreds of women through intention-based workshops and coaching. She inspires them to breathe life into their souls and align with their goals in both group and personal one-on-one settings. Kimberly believes that you should think of Love Your SoulSelf as an entry point to a new relationship with yourself.

She is a contributing author to the international best-selling book *365 Ways to Connect to Your Soul,* as well as the soon-to-be-released book *Goodness Abounds.* In addition, the story of how she was inspired to start the Love Your SoulSelf movement was featured in the book *Infinite Purpose.*

Kimberly has worked in the health-care industry for more than twenty years as a registered respiratory therapist and has also mastered many different holistic healing modalities. Her passion is helping women connect and embrace their true spirit while gaining trust and confidence in themselves by building on a foundation of self-love.

Connect with Kim:

Kim@loveyoursoulself.com

www.loveyoursoulself.com

facebook.com/loveyoursoulself

Chapter 10

FROM SHAME TO SHINE

The crack in my foundation came when I was eleven, when my dad left. Growing up with three older brothers, I was always surrounded by men, but it seemed when the patriarch left, all that was left was an unstable structure that crumbled under us. Existing on faulty ground at a pivotal point in my life left me feeling uneasy, and the world as I knew it shifted. Stable became unstable. Secure became insecure. Expected became unknown. Unconditional love became conditional. The family unit became broken. Trust became distrust, and pain, anger, resentment, disconnection, and loss came crashing in.

Unsure of how to cope with the plethora of emotions that were unknown to my peers and me, I looked for ways to numb what was swirling around inside. I started with antidepressants and sleeping aids and moved to bigger substances at the age of thirteen on a search to find a way to exist. I was feeling lost, so I turned to substance abuse as a way to connect with peers and it gave me something to look forward to. When I was numb, I didn't have to sit with the anger, pain, and feelings of being unworthy and insignificant. The drugs freed me from the feelings I had every time I looked into the mirror or closed my eyes. Day after day I gave all I had just to go through life, hoping that something would occur or change to give light to the deep, dark pit of my soul.

For a year that was how I woke up and went to sleep each night—numb and empty, feeling no control over my life. My future looked grim. I thought I would be dead by the age I am now writing this down. I had no hope for a brighter future. How could I just exist enough till it was time for me to go?

Making connections with people was difficult. How could I really, truly connect with someone else if I was so disconnected from myself? So at sixteen, when a man came into my life and I felt a connection, I was intrigued. He wasn't someone whom I would normally have been attracted to. But the energy around him made me feel safe and important, as if what I did mattered to him. At first it was little ways of making me feel safe, like picking me up from places so I wouldn't have to walk or always checking on me to make sure I was OK. Even just walking around with him, I felt I was in a safety bubble with him at my side.

What began with a feeling of safety, importance, and connection started to turn into control and manipulation. I was not able to dress a certain way or see certain people. I was unable to go certain places. Even my attending school was a reason for battle at times. The manipulation played over and over, day after day, in my head. I was told I would never be anything without him and I would never be good enough. No one else would ever love me. Every word pulled a little piece of me away from my truth. It became my reality. "If it was said, then it must be true," I thought. Everyone else must have seen it and thought that too, but he was the only one who had the guts to tell me the truth. The words broke me a little bit each day. They left me feeling powerless and defeated. But every so often, I would get a glimpse of light, a moment of strength, a time when my truth would squeeze its way from down deep inside of me to show me that this was not my reality and the situation I was in was not my path. That I was better and stronger and deserved more.

In those moments when my truth and my power within would show up, I would fight back. I would walk away and try to leave the relationship. Numerous times I tried and failed because the manipulation put the lid on my truth and my power. It was like a jack-in-the-box. Wind me up till I pop, then my power would bounce out, and then it would get shoved back down again—till one day I refused to allow it to be pushed back into the dark depths inside. No! I was holding my ground this time. In my soul I knew I was not what he was trying to make me become. I knew I had a choice: I could believe the manipulations or dig up some strength and stand in what little power I had left.

We came head-to-head - me trying to show up with what had been buried under the months of manipulation, and he trying to squash and get rid of every bit of my resistance. He knew I had found some strength and courage, and in his last attempt to vanquish all my power and have me truly give in, he forced himself on me, held me down, and raped me.

In that moment, he had won. I disconnected completely from the experience, as my struggle was not getting me anywhere. It felt as if I had left my body and was looking down on to what was occurring and waiting for it to end. In that moment I remember telling myself, "it will be OK. It won't last long. You can get through this." When it ended, what he took was what little power I had left. The numbness, unworthiness, pain, fear, shame, and guilt flooded my soul. I felt as if I were drowning in those emotions. But what was left was rage! And in that rage I knew I would never again allow him to get close enough to be able to do that to me and that somehow, some way, I would learn to survive and become complete again.

The fear prevented me from telling my family, the fear of what my dad or my brothers would do to him. What would happen to them if they killed him? Plus, what would they think of me if they knew? I feared people not believing me. How would they look at me? I didn't want to be known in school as the girl who was raped by her boyfriend. What would the other boys at school think? Would they think I was an easy target? If someone could do this to someone he supposedly loved, then what were my other relationships going to look like? Then came the shame and the guilt. I was ashamed of putting myself in that situation, of not being physically strong enough to fight him off or emotionally strong enough to get out of the relationship. I felt shame and guilt about my sexuality and about being a beautiful woman. So I developed a story in my head about the way I should be and came to the conclusion that I must not expose my sexuality, as that was unsafe.

This story and fear stayed with me for years in the background while I pretended it didn't exist. No one knew about that part of me, and it was buried so deep I thought it would never show up or impact me in the future. I truly disconnected myself from my sexuality, so much so that I avoided acknowledging that the rape affected me or had even occurred. It wasn't until I started my business, and my business and I continued to grow, that this deep, dark past started to peek through. I did not embrace or even see myself as a sexual woman. I would fear men even looking at me. The anxiety I had about sex with my husband was so strong at times that I would have full-blown panic attacks. It seemed the more I looked inward to self-discovery, loving my strengths, finding my truth, and allowing my true power to emerge again, the more this darkness would show up. The more I pretended it didn't affect me, the more it continued to knock at my door. I pushed it aside because I just didn't want to go there. "It isn't a big deal" is what I would tell myself every time.

On my quest for self-expansion, I found myself at a Game Changers Live event. That event changed everything. I could no longer hide. The moment I heard the story from one of the presenters about her sexual trauma and the impact that it had on her and how far she had come in her own journey of self-expansion was when I knew it was finally time to let it in. And it rushed in as if the dam in the river had just broken. The dam couldn't hold it in any longer. I grieved for about two weeks in bed, crying, journaling, and talking. It was in that time I told my mom what had happened. I told members of my team what had happened and let them see that side of me. I felt the need to expose this dark secret. I reflected on that time of my life, the pain, anger, and loneliness I had felt. I owned my part in the circumstance. I had hard conversations. I told my dad and my brothers, hearing their tears, because this was something they would never have wished on any woman, and it had occurred to a woman in their lives. The power that the story of the rape had had on me started to diminish. I was able to vanish the story of unworthy, insignificant, and unlovable around it; I was able to pull out the facts. The more people knew, the more it just became something that had occurred in my life, not something that determined how I would live my life.

In the process I have found my path—empowerment, freedom, love, and connection. The path to healing has been a journey. Before I started my business, I was a nurse, and now I see I was pulled down that path of healing others because at the time it was too difficult for me to heal myself. But assisting in others' healing was a step toward my path. Becoming an entrepreneur and all the personal expansion that goes along with that is what allowed me the tools to start to repair the crack in the foundation and stabilize the walls again. With a stronger structure, I am now able to share my story in hope that someone else gets the courage to share hers, to remove the power, shame, and guilt and expose the truth and beauty of the person who may be hiding underneath.

ABOUT MISSY A. GARCIA

Missy A. Garcia is keynote speaker, an author, and a passionate wellness advocate. Missy is driven to help women to break the mold of social norms and actively pursue the lives they truly desire: lives that are authentic to them as individuals and aren't limited by fear or circumstance.

Missy was trained as a nurse and had her mind opened to the idea of a more natural lifestyle during a holistic nursing program. But it wasn't until she became pregnant with her daughter in 2010 that her true holistic journey began.

During this time, Missy needed to find an alternative income stream that would support her family, and she began working as a network marketer and wellness advocate for doTERRA oils. This became a profitable entrepreneurial journey and pushed her out of her shell (as a self-proclaimed introvert) into leadership roles that challenged and transformed her.

Missy was confronted with the reality that she was living a life that was somewhat removed from her full potential and sought ways to break through fear, insecurity, and the obstacles of life's circumstances and find freedom and authenticity.

Missy is a powerful, inspirational speaker whose vision is to help women realize that they have the power within to create whatever life they desire.

"Happiness is not an illusion, but it comes from being truly in tune with, and connected to, the truth of who we are."

Connect with Missy:
Website: MissyAGarcia.com
E-mail: missy@missyagarcia.com
Facebook: @TheMissyAGarcia
Twitter: @MissyAGarcia   Instagram: @themissyagarcia

Chapter 11

THE ME I WAS MEANT TO BE

Everything happens for a reason. I have heard that statement at least a hundred times in my life, perhaps even a thousand times. But it has taken on new meaning for me as I've grown older. I did not know how true this statement was when I was twenty-five, but I have come to realize at age fifty-five that this phrase is truly one of my personal mantras. The pain I experienced in my lifetime allowed me to make a deeper connection to my soul and rise up to my own truth. My mother used to say, "What doesn't kill you makes you stronger." That definitely applied to my life. My journey provided me with gold nuggets—and with fool's gold too—and connected me to my true calling: my vocation as a life coach and manifest mentor.

Let me explain. I was born and raised in Alaska. I am the youngest of eight children, and I grew up in a close-knit Irish Catholic clan. My father died of a heart attack a month and half after I turned twenty-two, and less than four years later, my mother died of a stroke. I was twenty-five years old at the time, but honestly, I was twenty-five years young and too young to have lost both my parents. I felt like an orphan, and in essence, I truly was then.

I need to backtrack for a moment. I began to date at age sixteen, and rarely in my life had I not been in a relationship. Because I was raised Catholic, I had the dream to get married and live happily ever after, just like in the fairy tales. You know how the story goes in "Sleeping Beauty" or "Cinderella," where the womyn is saved by the man and lives a happily-ever-after life.

I was married in June, only a few short months after my mother had died in April. I thought this was the start of my fairy-tale life. Divorce was definitely not on my agenda, nor was it going to be part of my life experience. But seven years after my marriage began, I did get divorced.

It was my choice. My divorce served as the first step toward my finding out what it was I really wanted and who it was I really wanted to be. It may sound like a cliché, but it is true. For the first time in my life, I chose myself over the fairy-tale belief. I woke up one morning no longer happy or passionate about being married to my husband. I had experienced gut-wrenching pain several years earlier when I learned he had been unfaithful with several womyn I knew. It happened during the first year of our marriage. Often I see womyn blaming the other womyn for their husbands' infidelity, but I never felt that way, and I never understood why, because it was my husband who cheated.

I sought counseling to help me deal with my feelings of disappointment, anger, and sadness. It was through this Christian counseling I discovered compassion and forgiveness. I understood my husband was doing the best job he knew how to do with the tools and role models he had when he was growing up. He was not a bad person; he just made bad decisions. The counseling allowed me to see that I had fallen out of love with my husband and I had let go of the fairy-tale dream. It was OK for me to let go of my marriage and my belief in that fairy-tale life. It was time for me to end my marriage, and so I did.

Believing I had healed the sadness and pain caused from my first marriage, I quickly moved on and got remarried at thirty-five, less than two years after my divorce. I did not allow myself time to heal and reflect on my first marriage before getting into a second marriage. I thought that I was a survivor, strong and eager to move on. I was afraid to look within. I attracted the same scenario as I had in my first marriage with my second husband, except the unfaithfulness was not with womyn; it was with drugs—with crack cocaine, to be exact. My second husband took his own life a year and half after our wedding. I was devastated and a widow at thirty-six.

This was my second strong nudge toward finding out who I really was and what I really wanted. It was no longer about blaming my ex-husbands. I had called this forth. Through the pain of my second husband's death, I realized that just because someone needed me, it *did not* mean that it was love. I had confused need with love. In both marriages, I felt if I gave enough of the happy and loving wife, then my married life would be like the support and love I felt from my own family of origin and my love would make my husband's life better. Clearly, it did not in either case. It did not stop my first husband from cheating, and it did not stop my second husband from killing himself. I learned the hard way that love is not enough for an addict.

The corporate company I was working for moved me, now divorced and widowed, to North Carolina, where I spent a lot of time alone for the very first time in my adult life. As often as I could, I would walk or hike in the Blue Ridge Mountains, which were practically outside my back door. I remember when one of my sisters came to visit me and I said, "Here I am, thirty-seven and divorced, widowed, and with no children. I never thought in my wildest dreams that at this moment in time, I would be starting over. This is not what I imagined for myself at eighteen. I feel as if I have nothing to show for my life except two painful failed marriages." I soldiered on because that was all I knew how to do.

This was the beginning of my third chapter in finding myself.

Twelve years had gone by from my first marriage at age twenty-five to my second husband's death when I was thirty-seven. I remember going into the doctor's office and filling out an application that requested marital status and said, "Check each box that applies: Single, Married, Divorced, or Widowed." I was single, divorced, and widowed—three out of four. It was surreal.

I was aware at this time I needed to learn from my past, but I wasn't aware that things happen *for* you instead of *to* you so that you can discover *yourself*. I didn't realize that the universe and God were conspiring for me. Each marriage, each divorce, each death, each experience, each challenge, each painful event was an opportunity to connect with myself in a truly meaningful way.

At forty-four, the trajectory of my life was altered significantly by an autoimmune illness, and its root cause was heavy metal toxicity in my body. This illness kept me in bed for almost two and a half years. I was on a personal quest during this time to find healing and to create wholeness in my body, mind, and spirit. This put me in my fourth chapter in finding myself. It was in this chapter of my life that I sought out answers and remedies for my illness. My illness was threefold I learned. I was not just physically ill but also emotionally and spiritually ill. I wanted to understand these things to make sure they would never happen again. Using different healing modalities, I learned how to rise up to connect with the love inside myself. Finding out why this illness had occurred allowed me to get to know me, myself, and I. I discovered that the body can and will heal with the right resources. I believe in wholeness and I believe in miracles, and both of these occurred in my life and in my body.

I awoke during this period of my life to realize that all those things I had experienced (both good and bad) up until then were my journey to discover myself. All the physical pain and emotional challenges became opportunities for me to get to know myself so that I could rise up to my authentic self. During this time, I connected to my purpose and to my passion about why I was put here on earth. That purpose is to help other womyn connect to their power sources so we can rise up together to shift the vibration of humanity into a brighter light. We all have a purpose to step into, and the journey is to become awake enough to rise up to it.

ABOUT TALLY HAYDEN

Tally Hayden is the founder of We Rise Coaching. She is a manifest mentor, certified life coach, published columnist, soulpreneur, wellness advocate, sales trainer, and professional speaker.

A lover of nature and sunsets, she was born and raised in Alaska as the youngest of eight children. She grew up fishing, hiking, camping, and playing basketball and softball in one of the rainiest climates in the United States—in Juneau, the capital of Alaska.

Her tenacious, loving spirit thrives by helping people connect to their power within and especially by helping womyn reconnect to their soul's purpose. She has a successful business background as a former chief operations officer (COO), owner and creator of a historic bed-and-breakfast, sales and marketing executive and consultant, trainer, election supervisor, state legislative aide, and congressional staff member. She owned and operated a successful Awaken Higher Brain Living™ Center in Milwaukee, Wisconsin.

She is happily married to a man she often calls her Dreamy Guy, who lovingly supported her through her journey to successfully heal herself from an autoimmune disease.

Tally is passionate about raising the vibration of humanity to live more fully in joy, laughter, peace, purpose, and passion. She created a free guide titled *Manifesting Your Life: 5 Do's and Dont's*, which can be downloaded from her website. You may also schedule a complimentary coaching session with her.

Contact Tally through her website at TallyHayden.com.

Chapter 12

YOUR GREATEST RESISTANCE
REVEALS YOUR BIGGEST REWARD

Terror flooded my whole body as the technician went silent, and the energy of the room went still. Everything went into slow motion. My eyesight blurred, and my hearing went fuzzy. I tried with all my strength to keep smiling, to keep the small talk flowing in an effort to protect my husband and prolong my own denial. But I already knew the truth. I raised my head and looked into my husband's eyes. His fear was barely contained. He had felt it too.

Something was dreadfully wrong.

I was twenty weeks pregnant with our second child. We were at my mid-pregnancy ultrasound appointment. With the excitement of learning whether we would have a boy or a girl, it never even crossed our minds that something could—or would—be wrong. Our two-year-old daughter, our firstborn, was a magical whirlwind of vivacious and precocious energy. She was beautiful, smarter than both of us put together, and the absolute picture of health. Our family history, on all sides, was remarkably healthy. We just never saw it coming. And just like that, our white-picket world was wildly out of control, tilted profoundly off balance and spinning us into the unknown.

We were devastated to learn during the ultrasound that our unborn son had a life-threatening heart defect. And that wasn't the end of the frightening news: we were told that these types of defects were often teamed with chromosome abnormalities, such as Down syndrome. The doctor who read the results of the ultrasound felt the findings were so dire that he suggested we might want to consider aborting the pregnancy, at twenty weeks.

In those very first moments, before more tests, before a second opinion...abort the pregnancy. How, in a matter of minutes, did we go from the elation of learning the sex of our unborn child, and feeling all the emotions parents feel when considering the brightness of their child's future, to considering the inconsiderable?

I already knew this child inside of me. He was kicking; he was growing; he was already a part of our family; he was already my son. How was I expected to even consider the option?

Devastation, shock, fear, and heartbreak settled in and quickly took root.

The slowness in which the next couple of weeks seemed to move was absolute agony. Waiting for test results of this magnitude was sheer torture. It was hard to focus on anything else. I mourned the loss of normalcy. I dove deep into the "why mes." I felt myself resist with all my might these next required steps into the unknown: the giving up of control. The feelings of helplessness were overwhelming and not something I was comfortable getting used to. I honestly didn't know what to do with myself. I found myself imagining scenarios of every outcome, trying with all my might to be prepared for anything and everything. Trying to control the uncontrollable to calm the worry.

When the results finally came in, we were overwhelmingly relieved to learn that there were no findings of chromosome abnormalities, no Down syndrome. Unfortunately, we soon learned after another round of tests that his heart complications were far more serious than they had first suspected.

Owen was born by cesarean section to save him from too much strain during birth. I remember them calling out his weight—five pounds, six ounces—and feeling the flood of worry hit me in a whole-new way. So small, so fragile. Am I ready for this? They whisked him off to the neonatal intensive-care unit (NICU) for testing and observation before I got a chance even to see his precious little face or hold his frail little body.

Because of the extreme circumstances, the very first time I saw my son's face was in a photograph. I was grateful to see he was OK, but it felt raw and strange to "meet" my son in this way. The nurses were so kind and thoughtful, knowing how anxious I was feeling not being able to see, let alone touch, my son. When I was cleared from the recovery room but still not able to leave my bed, they wheeled me down to the NICU. I could tell this wasn't quite normal protocol, by their nervous giggles and their continued assurances that it was "fine," as they weaved me through all the cribs and beeping machines to get me close enough to see Owen with my own eyes. Such a beautiful thing to do. It really touched me.

A few hours later, Owen was cleared from the NICU, and I was finally able to hold my beautiful boy for the first time. The connection was instant. There was no doubt in my heart that this boy was meant to be here, with us, right here, right now... and always.

For the first few weeks of Owen's life, we all adjusted to having a newborn in the house. Most of the time, it was business as usual with an almost three-year-old running the show. My daughter, Areia, wasn't thrilled about the idea of having a brother, particularly the amount of mama time he was stealing from her. She made thoughtful suggestions as three-year-olds often do: "We should toast him in the toaster with the bagels" and "Perhaps we could send him to the zoo to live with the monkeys." The usual adjustments were made (but nothing ever as extreme as her suggestions!). I tried very hard, but not very successfully, to hide my fear and my stress from her, from everyone, to push on, to be strong, but the uncertainty and the unknown were consuming me.

After many trips to the hospital to understand what exactly was happening with Owen's heart, the doctors told us that without a series of surgeries, our son wouldn't survive childhood. His heart would fail him by the time he was ten, maybe twelve. I don't think it really, truly hit me, the extreme severity of his condition, until I heard those words.

He wouldn't live past childhood if we didn't take invasive action. Can you imagine having to choose to put your child's life at such an extreme risk so you could save him?

Neither could I.

The doctors proposed a plan. The first open-heart surgery would be scheduled when my son was six months old to prep his heart for the massively complicated overhaul they would need to perform when he was a year old. Everything was discussed, decided, and agreed on. For six months we would wait…but, as I'm sure you know, in these sort of extreme circumstances, things rarely go as planned. When Owen was just six weeks old, his heart began to fail. He was suffering from frequent episodes of **tachycardia. His heart would beat far too fast**, like he was sprinting for his life, and his body wasn't able to stop the episodes on its own. It was causing a massive strain on his fragile condition.

The surgery that was scheduled for when he was a year old couldn't wait.

He was dying.

I took a total free-fall dive into the dark recesses of my mind. Fear, frantic fear, consumed me. I felt helpless; I felt powerless; I felt terrified. My walls went up. I shut down. I wanted to be completely disengaged from this consuming reality that was now my life. I didn't know whether I could push through this. I didn't know whether I had the strength it was going to take to hold him up, to hold myself up, to hold everyone up—to get *everyone* through this. How could I possibly do this?

I've always been the type of person who gets it done on my own, no need for help.

Push; push; push. Keep the walls up. Figure it out on your own. Make it work. Be strong!

Never let the shell of perfection be cracked! Never let your guard down.

THE FIRST GLIMPSE

But as hard as I fought, my shell of perfection received its first of many mighty cracking blows—and thankfully, it would never quite fully recover. Letting go of control, accepting support and guidance, and letting my guard come crumbling down was the beginning of something positively life changing.

I remember a key moment, a key shift that would eventually awaken me to the fact that *we aren't meant to do this alone, and we are stronger together*, which has become a major theme in my present teachings.

My mom shared with me that my grandmother had asked her church congregation to pray for little Owen, her great-grandson, to heal him and to keep us all strong through his upcoming surgeries. My mom also shared that, in fact, many, many people in our community (these were the days before the social-media explosion) had expressed their concern and were sending their love and prayers for Owen and for all of us. People who had never met Owen. People who had never met my husband or me. Complete strangers. Complete strangers willing to openly share their love and light to help heal my baby boy and hold all of us up in our time of need.

The relief, the gratitude, washed over me like a warm wave of lightness. I could feel the power of their thoughts and prayers. I could feel them all collectively holding us up, sending their powerful healing energy to us all:

You don't have to do this on your own. Lean in. We've got you. We've got all of you.

The realization was absolute relief. I didn't have to hold everything and everyone up alone, and in fact, I never was doing it alone—any of it, ever. My walls had just grown so thick and guarded that I wasn't allowing myself to receive the miracles or see the magic that surround us every day, in every way. This realization began to soften my edges. It allowed me to feel *hope* in a whole-new way—and hope I did, with everything I had. Through the next six weeks, *hope* was my everything. Even through talks of potential heart transplants and 70 percent success rates and signing forms acknowledging that our son may die of surgical complications, it helped me focus on the *knowing* that Owen was going to be OK.

OPEN FOR MIRACLES

All through the first surgery, I held Owen's baby blanket to my heart, smelled it, and caressed it. I held a photo of him that I prayed to, telling him to be strong, that we were right there with him.

I envisioned over and over again him graduating high school and tossing his hat in the air. I watched him walking, so proudly, down the aisle with his beautiful bride. I saw his children, my grandchildren, running toward me and jumping into my arms. Over and over for hours, I held strong to the faith that he would live a long, strong, healthy life and that we would all be together as a family for a very, very long time.

After six hours the surgeon emerged. He had amazing news. They had made all the mind-baffling repairs, basically replumbed and rewired Owen's tiny little heart, and when they took him off life support and restarted his heart (yes, his heart was not beating for six hours), they found it functioning far better than any of their *highest* expectations. It truly was a miracle. I was flooded over with gratitude for this man, for his team. They had saved our son's life. They had given all of us a second chance at happiness. They had rewritten the course of our lives. The relief and gratitude were immeasurable.

THE AWAKENING

Over the next four weeks, Owen's recovery was not without its own battles. He would survive a life-threatening blood infection and endure one more surgery to install his permanent pacemaker. Things were still raw and unpredictable. But as he began to awaken from four weeks of induced slumber and I was allowed to hold him for the first time in as many weeks, I didn't know it yet, but I had begun to awaken for the first time too.

As Owen became stronger and was nearing a full recovery, I began to feel myself noticing things with a much stronger sense of clarity. Before I even knew what a "gratitude practice" was, I began to see life through more grateful lenses. I began to realize that even in my darkest moments, it's possible that someone else has it much, much worse. We were being given a second chance with our son; he would come home with us in less than a week, just in time to celebrate his first Christmas. We would get to watch him grow and turn into the amazing man he was meant to be. The gift we were being given was not lost on me. Every day at the hospital, I would see parents who were fighting for one more day with their precious child. One more hug, one more smile, one more kiss. One more chance to see their child's sparkly eyes shining back at them.

One more day, please, just one more day.

My pain did not cross that threshold. I'm eternally grateful to have the gift of Owen every day of my life.

THE SPARK RELIT

It would take another two years for life to truly begin to settle. Owen steadily grew stronger and more stable, and as he did, my world slowly began to open up again. When you are in the thick of it, consumed by whatever crisis you are experiencing, your head is down, your focus is concise, and it can be really difficult to emerge from that place of fear and worry even after the dust settles and the prognosis is good.

I felt myself begin to lift my head and consider my life for the first time in a long time. I began to (and finally could) consider my life as someone other than "the mom of a sick child." It's easy to let the stories and experiences of your life continue to define you. It's also easy to fall into the *comfort zone* of playing a role that has been given to you.

I had become suddenly aware that I was still clinging unnecessarily to the role of "the mom of a sick child" out of fear of the unknown and what was next for me.

I knew it was time to let it go and move forward, for my son's healing and for mine.

This experience had stirred an awakening in me and began the process of *coming home to myself.*

ASK AND YOU SHALL RECEIVE

I needed *something.*

I wasn't sure what it was…but I knew in my heart I needed *SOMETHING*…and looking back, the dots are so clearly connected. With this need, I was inadvertently asking the Universe to show me the answer…and it did.

So when I looked up on that fateful day during that *"I need something"* phase, I saw it. Top shelf, easy to miss, but there it was, the book that would forever fill my *"I need something"* void.

This book brought it all together for me. It felt as if everything I had been experiencing and exploring but hadn't quite been able to put into words was all right here, explained. I was so completely intrigued and inspired I could hardly contain it. This new understanding, this new comprehension, this new way of being—it tied so many things together for me.

I had asked for *something*, and the universe responded by waltzing the magic of *fêng shui* into my life—and I began to dance. It was exactly what I needed, and I was hooked.

I've always been fascinated by interior spaces and interior design, so much so that I have made it my vocation of choice since earning degrees in architecture and interior design in college. But this book took what I already intuitively knew about our living spaces and how they profoundly affect us beyond our logical understanding and put it into words for me. The fact that we can actually *connect* and *manifest* our desires by tapping into the universal energy through our homes and living spaces absolutely blew my mind in the most beautiful way. Imagine, just as you plug in and download knowledge using the Internet, you can plug in and manifest your dreams using your living environment. I began to think of my home as my very own request hotline. What an incredible gift I had been given!

My desire to expand and explore this newfound tool began to awaken my spirit. I felt inspired. It made me curious about my life in a way I had never felt before. I wanted to uncover the answers. I wanted to understand what was holding me back, what was keeping me locked down, what was keeping me from fully removing my shell—and now, thanks to my understanding of fêng shui, I could *see* my life, my blocks, my self-limiting beliefs, my unhealthy patterns, and how they presented themselves, fully manifested in my home. I wanted to know what steps I needed to take to begin to fully flourish and succeed in my life. This was my pathway, my tool, to create ease and freedom in my life. I could finally *do something* to create change in my life, and *change* it did.

THE DETOUR BECOMES THE PATH

The knowledge I was able to access through the connection I created with the methods of fêng shui provided me with profound *clarity* again and again. Practicing fêng shui was opening my eyes and my world in ways I hadn't imagined possible. It helped me to continue to peck at and slowly remove my shell of perfectionism. It helped me realize that I had been afraid to fully connect with the richness inside of me out of fear of what it may uncover and lead me toward—something that wasn't safe, that wasn't perfect, or even…*gasp*…messy. I had locked myself down, preferring to stay safe, creating a thick shell around me and an illusion of control. I had been afraid to uncover and reveal my gifts, even to myself, for fear of judgment, disrespect, and ridicule. The energy I was creating in my home with the power of fêng shui helped me peel back the layers that had been built up over a lifetime of fear and helped lead me to the understanding that embracing my softness, my vulnerabilities, and my uniqueness in its truest form was actually the path to success.

Practicing fêng shui plugged me back in. It helped me connect, listen, and understand my higher power and my inner wisdom. The connection opened my eyes to the miracles that surround us every day. I call them *soul snaps,* those universal detours, coincidences, or serendipitous events that wake us up with a *snap* and push us down the path toward our true passion and the joy of fully living in our purpose.

By continuing to follow those *soul snaps*, just as when my eyes locked on to the book that would change my life, it became abundantly clear to me that my true path was to help women who struggle within the confines of their own fear and their own restrictions of familiarity.

My path was to help awaken their path's. To guide them towards discovering their own passion and purpose.

Most of my clients seek my services for one of two reasons: either they've encountered a very loud *soul snap*, it's become abundantly clear that *something is missing...*and their path to awakening can't wait a minute longer!

Or they have begun on a path of self-discovery, perhaps fueling their entrepreneurial spirit, but they keep coming up against *blocks* or self-limiting beliefs that make them feel as if *progress* is no longer a word in their vocabulary. They are seeking ways to achieve more ease, freedom, and abundance in their lives and businesses.

For my client's this process is an awakening, just like my own. "Aha!" moments are everywhere they look. It's beautiful to watch. I help them get curious, in a new way, just as I did, about what is blocking their lives, their businesses, and their access to happiness, wealth, love, and success. Together, with the methods of fêng shui and my ability to read their homes and intuitively look more deeply into the underlying issues they are pushing up against, their lives are propelled forward with a momentum I wish I could have wrangled when I was first on this path!

It takes courage to become open to the possibilities that are ever present and waiting for us to grasp. Sometimes it takes an intervention of massive proportions, like an illness or almost losing a child, to access this courage. Taking those first extremely shaky steps out of my safety zone was a huge challenge for me, like the universe drawing a line in the sand and daring me to cross. If I hadn't, I would have never uncovered my intuitive abilities or discovered my true gift, my true joy, of helping women on their own paths to awakening and self-discovery. The more challenges you accept, the more you grow, the more aligned you feel. Continuing to shatter old patterns and self-limiting beliefs will keep your energy fully flowing. Every breakthrough you achieve is an expanded awakening, helping you feel more empowered and vital, helping you feel alive for the first time—again and again.

I use fêng shui every day in my life to create miracles and access clarity around any issue I'm encountering. It is an incredibly powerful way to connect the dots and see what's working and what's not working. Whatever you desire, this tool gives you direct insight into why it hasn't shown up yet. Whether it's a loving partner, or a more intimate relationship, or a steady flow of clients. Or opportunities for more ease, flow, freedom, and success. Whatever you desire, fêng shui is your direct request hotline to the universe.

Here are a few examples of how fêng shui can work for you:

Are you struggling to invite a new love into your life? Let's take a closer look at your bedroom. First, make sure that you aren't displaying photos of an *old* love or an *ex*-love. The energy of your space and the things you choose to put in it are always influencing you subconsciously. If your space is occupied by symbols of an old, hurtful love, then your life will be occupied by the same. Out with the old, in with the new! Second, take a closer look and see whether you are displaying art that is singular in nature, meaning photos of you alone or a painting of a woman standing alone, longingly looking off into the distance. Our subconscious is directly connected to the energy of the universe. The energy of the universe is a very literal creature and follows your lead. Fêng shui teaches you to look at your spaces with very literal eyes to see what you are actually manifesting, not what you *hope* you are manifesting. Adding photos and artwork of loving couples enjoying each other will enhance and emphasize your intention to call in a loving, fulfilling relationship. Third, take a look at your bed. Is one side pushed up against the wall? Make room for your new love physically by pulling the bed away from the wall and granting him or her access to your space and your heart. You can also open up space in your closet and clear out a drawer for his or her things. Fourth, whether you are looking for love or are in a current relationship, create space for an equal partnership. Create equal access to both sides of the bed as well, adding equally sized bedside tables, lamps, and accessories. If you begin to take these steps, you will see results. This new insight and inspiration is already beginning the shift, sending out a ripple of intention, which leads to change. Your physical actions will seal the deal.

I will leave you with one more transformational fêng shui tip. If you are struggling to invite new abundance opportunities into your life, such as a steady stream of clientele or successful business ventures, take a look at your desk. Do you have a desk or a space where you do business? Having a defined *business* space is crucial if you want to be defined as an entrepreneur that should be taken seriously. Make sure your desk is cleared. If your desk always has a pile of papers and mess, then there is no room to invite new opportunities and no place to put them. Having your desk cleared not only keeps the opportunities flowing in but also helps you stay clear, focused, and on purpose.

This is just the beginning. Of course, there are many layers to fêng shui and the work that I do, but this is a great example of how you can easily begin to incorporate some of the magic and see the results for yourself. If your curiosity is piqued, I invite you to join me for a complimentary Fêng Shui Mini Course, which will launch you forward on your path of self-discovery and open your eyes to the possibilities that are fully available to you. Get started here: http://www.jenheilman.com/awaken

I appreciate your support so very much. So for you, my beautiful book reader, I have a gift just for you: follow this link www.jenheilman.com/inspire and enter the password INSPIRE to unlock your free gift! Enjoy the awakening!

ABOUT JEN HEILMAN

Jen Heilman is a fêng shui expert, an intuitive and transformational coach, the creator of the Abundance Academy, and a mamapreneur on a mission. She teaches soulful women entrepreneurs how to use the amazingly effective power of fêng shui to access clarity, inspiration, and success in their lives and businesses.

Jen helps women around the globe awaken their souls, unleash their passion and purpose, and step into the power and beauty that are uniquely their own. She accomplishes this through one-on-one coaching, group coaching programs like the Abundance Academy, online programs, live workshops, webinars, and guest-expert speaking events.

Jen graduated from Vermont Technical College with an associate of applied science in architecture and building engineering technology. She then transferred to Montana State University, where she earned a bachelor of arts in interior design. She has also earned a certificate of graduation in fêng shui interior design from the Sheffield School of Design in New York City.

She has been an interior and architectural designer for twenty years and a fêng shui practitioner for ten years. She has always been fascinated by spatial design and the undeniable power it has to make us feel safe, supported, and *at home* within ourselves.

Jen now shares her fêng shui knowledge, intuitive skills, and life experiences with her students and clients to help propel their lives forward with profound momentum. To learn more about how you can connect with Jen and experience your own transformation, please visit her website at www.JenHeilman.com.

To get a glimpse of the transformative experience you'll have with Jen, please go to her website and sign up for the complimentary Fêng Shui Challenge and embrace the magic of "getting your *SHWAY* on!" at http://www.jenheilman.com/5daychallenge.

Website: www.JenHeilman.com

E-mail: jen@jenheilman.com

Facebook Business Page: @thejenheilman

Facebook Personal Page: www.facebook.com/jenheilman

Facebook Group- www.facebook.com/groups/ Designyourlifewithfengshui

Instagram: @jenheilman   Twitter: @jen_heilman

Chapter 13

TRAVEL WITH YOUR SOUL MAP

You are the universe! Sun, moon, planets, and stars are in your body. Yes, you have that in you. The way I know this is because I have studied and experienced it from the point of view of vibrational science, medicine, acupuncture, coaching, and spiritual experience. At the end, the truth is one; only in order for us to accept it and comprehend it, we need to see it through different lenses. If you are reading this chapter, I know one thing about you for sure: I know that you have an important job to do on this planet, you have become aware of it, and now you are ready to do it. I am grateful for the opportunity to add a few more signs on that path.

No matter what you say or believe today, I absolutely know that your gifts are far beyond what you know, no matter how much you already live them. How do I know that? I have learned that from intelligence much bigger than you and me together, and I call it simply *universe*. I also learned that we write our soul maps based on what our souls want to experience and grow from. We also consciously choose our souls' journeys what gifts we are here to share, how we want to serve with our light, and the virtues we want to embrace through different relationships.

But hold on: you might say, "This sounds too good to be true!" Well, yes, but no one said it was going to be a safe ride. We all agreed before we were born that we were coming for adventures for our souls and to bring heaven to earth. So whatever other plan you have in your mind, it might not unfold as you think. As Woody Allen said, "If you want to make God laugh, tell him about your plans."

QUAOAR—A MIRACULOUS EVENT

I have always believed that everything is somehow meaningfully connected, but I could never have guessed that the discovery of a faraway object in space would change the direction of my life.

In October 2002 I was invited to attend a lecture about a newly discovered object in the Kuiper Belt called Quaoar. At the time I was busy working for a pharmaceutical company, but I was just starting to learn about the decisions we make beyond the control of our logical mind. Although I wanted to turn down the invitation, and I was just preparing to say no to this invitation, something inside of me was faster than my logical mind, and I heard myself saying, "I will be there." That was the first surprise; I couldn't understand why I had agreed to go when I had no interest in this topic. When the day arrived, I still didn't understand why I should go there, but I jumped to my feet, got dressed, and drove to the place. I was almost angry with myself, but more than that I was confused, as I didn't understand what was going on. While I was waiting for the lecture, the voices in my head started getting louder and demanding an explanation as to why I was there wasting my time. When the lecture started, a man (today my husband and my soul mate, Alex) came on stage and started talking about the newly discovered object and it's meaning on a global level and in our personal lives. My mind became silent, and I felt complete peace in my heart. Alex was talking about the meaning of the newly discovered sky object Quaoar in our personal life. This native Indian god is destroying all worlds below his feet by dancing, but he is happy. He knows that after chaos, a new world will emerge. And it means in our personal life that if we come here to hear this story, we are ready for the new expansion of consciousness.

Nothing made sense to my logical mind, but I felt tremendous gratitude. A deep gentle voice that I had never heard before told me that I had received the sign to open my soul map and my gifts. And I did. I quit my corporate job, I start traveling, and I lived in Italy, and then I decided to stay in the United States and started living in Marina del Rey, Los Angeles. It is interesting synchronicity as this is the area from where mythology of native Indian God of destruction and creation comes from. I managed to build there a life that looked perfect to everyone else. Only one thing was missing: I was not alive or happy. To be honest, I was so depressed that one day I was not able to deny it anymore. So I stopped and faced the first issue—I was not in love with my fiancé. Once I admitted that, many other issues started surfacing as well. The truth was ugly and painful, but so clear—my life was perfect picture from outside, while inside was different.

So what to do then? I held my breath and jumped into the swimming pool and swam alone for more than an hour. I wasn't planning anything. I just surrendered, and after many laps, I started feeling that presence and peace again. When I came out of that swimming pool, I was in deep peace and clarity, and I knew I was not living my life from my heart and that was going to change now. I was ready to start dancing with the god of destruction and creation. I said yes and he said OK and started removing everything from my life that does not serve me anymore. Just one year after the Quaoar lecture, I lived in California for six months, and in another six months, I faced the deaths of people close to me—my fiancé died suddenly, and my friend got deathly sick but managed to survive. I lost a few close friends whom I needed to let go of, and I changed my religion, my name, my home, and my profession. It was painful and scary. And I become live and present. I built my new world based on truth, on my real heart values, on my dreams, and on *love.*

How did I make this change? Basically two things: listening to my soul during meditation and walking on my soul map. What do I mean by soul map? I believe that horoscope of a person viewed from soul perspective is the best map to organize your life around your purpose. So I made decisions according to my map—to leave my company, to leave the medical field and my specialization in a prestigious research center, and to step into the world of the esoteric science of astrology. I never planned this, but my soul called me. And I was managing better and better a connection with that deep silence and soul-map navigation. After releasing many layers of old, limiting beliefs, I could see that the creation god Quaoar was put in my path to prepare me deeply for the next level of my life journey. Archetypes of gods and goddesses that are crossing our life path in the form of mythological stories and symbols are powerful signs from our higher being, telling us that it is time to align stronger with our life purpose. I didn't plan for any of this to be part of my life, but I let go and I let God and universe in. From that place my life became magical. I started talking with universe with the cosmic language of hermetic astrology, and I was receiving signs, guidance, and resources so easily. I was on my soul-map journey, and I knew that deep in my heart, without any doubt.

So the magic dust spread in my life. I got married to my soul mate, Alex, on Magic Island in Hawaii, and we traveled almost one year all over the world, even selling our apartment. We had each other, and we were on a mission to open up space in ourselves and to connect soul to soul. When we were ready, we came back home with a clear vision to share our knowledge with others in need, and we opened an international institute for astrology education and research, the first one in our country and all the Balkans. It was really a pioneer act, and we got a lot of media attention. Some recognized how deep and serious our work was; some called us a Harry Potter school, but with a clear intention and an open heart, we managed to attract amazing students from all walks of life.

I was so in love and felt so alive. For many years I tried to figure out how to blend all my different interests in medicine, quantum physics, esotery, and spirituality. The guidance came together in a perfect and authentic blend once I stopped trying and started listening. These things all had one common denominator—me. When I began my master's degree, I wanted to work on the brain, but instead I was driven to work on the electromagnetic field of the heart. I now see I was guided to this path. Later I had resistance to work on solar spots, but that knowledge brought me to better understand astrology and its influence on human behavior. My work in the field of human physiology and electromagnetic fields in the human body blended with my yoga knowledge to open my eyes to the fact that the electromagnetic fields along our spines are chakras. Each chakra is connected with one planet in our horoscopes. It was clear to me that from a scientific and esoteric view, we are vibrational beings first and earth is a living being too. All this was food for my soul, enjoying the chance to put puzzles together. Working more on this, I realized that the hermetic maxim that we are microcosms is not philosophy but a real thing. It means that our brain looks exactly like a solar system but in micro version and that our universe looks like a network of human neurons in micro version. I also started noticing synchronicity and connections in discoveries about the brain and the cosmos. Every time a neuroscientist made a breakthrough in knowing more about the human brain, a shift and discovery happened in knowing and seeing more in the cosmos. I started teaching people, even on national TV, about the connection between the dark parts of our brains and dark matter in the cosmos. I was so happy, but I knew something was missing. I was reading and learning more, but I still knew something was missing that would connect the dots.

GET OUT OF YOUR SHELL

In order for us to find the missing core parts, we need to get out of our shells completely when the right time comes. Becoming more requires stepping into more light. That requires going to the deepest parts of ourselves, where we safely hide our most vulnerable parts. But at some point, we need to stop running away and start hugging the parts of us that the world was not ready to know. We all have parts of us that we believe are too intense, too wild, too original, or too different, so we decided we needed to control them and hide them. So they become our shadows and missing parts on our soul journeys. But one day, in order to complete our puzzles and see the whole picture, we need to go down there to find these missing pieces.

At this point in my life, I have gone out of my comfort zone and changed my old beliefs in many different ways to pursue my truth, and I have become strong by living my life according to my heart. But sometimes one kind and gentle act of soul-to-soul recognition can shake the world stronger than an earthquake. I went one beautiful spring day to a new acupuncture office, and without any lead-in, the doctor asked me, "Can you see auras?"

As I was unprepared for the question, I honestly said, "Yes."

She asked, "Can you look at mine and tell me more about my aura?" I was so surprised I just obeyed her. I closed my eyes so I could clearly see the color in and around her body, and then I started describing the color that I saw in her aura and what it usually meant. In the violet color around the second chakra, I was seeing a lot of time with people who were skilled at painting.

She smiled, nodding her head, and said, "I want to show you my pictures. I love to paint." She took me to another office and showed me her pictures, and she said, "I am so happy that I can share this with you." All this happened fast, and after ten minutes, she said, "Thank you so much," and hugged me.

I needed to leave, as she had another client. I don't know why, but I started walking fast to reach my car as soon as I could. Once

I sat in the car, I started to cry. I was crying from my stomach and solar plexus like a little child; my entire body was shaking. All that was suppressed came to surface. All these memories from when I was a child seeing so much more than others around me, feeling so much more, and not knowing what to do with it. And the incredible effort I put into trying to fit in, being excellent in so-called valuable things that I had no interest in at all, like math and history. But no matter what I did, I knew inside of me that I was not normal, which means I am different, and that was so scary for that little girl. So she tried to hide. But now, when this doctor who first time saw me and recognized me from my being, all became clear to me, but from some different perspective, it felt like I was looking on myself from above and seeing the big picture. In that moment I realized that this was prenatal decision of my soul. I could clearly see gifts that came from it. I stopped crying and started laughing from my heart and whole body, feeling deep relaxation in all my muscles. I could feel the flow in my spine as a rushing, joyful river of life. I discovered that day another part of my purpose puzzle I am here: to help others deep dive and find missing pieces of themselves so they can shine fully.

ADJUSTING WITH THE VIBRATION OF YOUR SOUL— BODY INTELLIGENCE AND EASY MANIFESTATION

Once I unlocked the pillar of light in my body, my perception changed. I started clearly seeing energy patterns in my clients. Whatever they wanted to change outside came from their need to restore the glow of light in their bodies. To help, I built a system of fast energy diagnostics and healing so people can see for themselves where the body is blocked and how it is manifesting in their physiology, beliefs, thoughts, emotions, and life circumstances. Once they can see it, they are ready to change it. I realized that when we try to prevent the expression of a certain emotion, it will always be accompanied by a blockage or spasm in a certain body part. The release of emotions liberates the body, and the same is true for the reverse process. So I was able to create (or better, download) these energy exercises that help release emotions and awaken the energy in certain energy centers, the *chakras*.

When people release feelings of guilt and the need to be perfect and constantly improve themselves from the second chakra, below the umbilicus, wonderful results happen. They not only find partners und value themselves more, but others start to value them differently as well. This allows them to relax in that feeling of pleasure without guilt, often creating more income and more free time. Working more and more with myself and others, I have noticed that the heart chakra is where each of us needs to return to more often. Once the heart chakra opens, I see people discover their purpose and incorporate healthy habits with no effort. But most importantly, they start seeing themselves from the soul's perspective and recognize the once-hidden parts as core gifts that they start organizing businesses and relationships around.

YOU ARE NOT NORMAL—YOU ARE AMAZING

So this work finds its path to go into the world. It seems that the joy we have in our work is the best catalyst for growing. In my educational and coaching groups enter astrologers, psychologists, yoga teachers, healers, and many different coaches. It unfolds into live workshops in energy astrology and astrohealing. Amazing results and joy spread, and I got invitations from many different countries to speak about it. And it developed into an international school with students and clients all over the world. My life was not going by my rational plan; it goes on the heart-and-soul track. It brings me amazing people to cocreate with.

Today I know after working with so many people from different walks of life that we are all souls and we are all tender and full of love inside. We are all able to see and hear more when we allow that to ourselves. I believe as you read this that you are ready to activate your soul map and your core gifts. We are all avatars, and no one is really normal. We are all amazing and extraordinary. We are not here to reject anything; we are here to accept more of who we are and to live it consciously. Remember, the best plan is the one you travel from your soul script.

ABOUT DR. LEA IMSIRAGIC

Dr. Lea Imsiragic is an international speaker, author, astrologer and intuitive success coach. She blends her expertise in human physiology, acupuncture, energy psychology, flower essences, coaching and astrology to help people discover their most amazing and deepest gifts and live them fully in all areas of their lives.

After working with thousands of clients and students all over the world, she created an accurate energy and astrological system for diagnosis and therapy: energy astrology certification training and coaching, astromeridians, and astrohealing.

Lea is the author of six books about astrology and vibrational health, cofounder of the Kepler Institute for Astrological Research and Education, and president of the Association for Energy Psychology in Belgrade, Serbia. She also runs online distance-learning programs..

Lea's biggest passion is teaching people how to practically live the truth that they are the universe and how to build amazing life and business around this truth. She and her husband Aleksandar travel the world sharing her message. Lea's books have been translated into English, Russian, and Turkish.

Connect with Lea here:

lea@keplerunited.org

leaimsiragic.com

Visit http://www.leaimsiragic.com/freegift to get immediate access to the energy astrology test for your chakras.

Chapter 14

LESSONS FROM THE CORE

"**M**ommy, are you going to workie?"

"Yes."

"Why are you going to workie?"

"Because I have people waiting for me who need to do Pilates."

"How long will you be gone?"

"Only one class tonight."

"Can you give them only one exercise?"

"Yes, baby, only one, and then I will come in and snuggle with you as soon as I get home."

"Promise you'll only give them one exercise and not five exercises, because I really want to snuggle with you."

That was how my evenings would begin. My short drive to the studio was filled with anxiety, upset stomach, aches, pains, tears, mom guilt, business-owner guilt, and the constant stress of having one foot in and one foot out. I always assumed it must have felt much like a bad marriage, one that you always contemplate leaving. The weight of being stuck was always there.

My entrepreneurial journey began as a passion to help others improve their posture and decrease pain and ultimately allowed me to help heal others through Pilates and fitness. I originally started taking Pilates myself in 2000, to rehab chronic low-back pain. Scans of my spine showed herniated, bulging discs and spinal stenosis. I decided then and there that I would find an exercise program and a *bigger* purpose to strengthen my body and not succumb to the negative aspects associated with chronic pain. In the beginning, my Pilates practice and being a studio owner gave me all that and more. However, over time, what started as a leap of faith had turned into a burden rather than a blessing. I was depleted, and not only could I not help others in the capacity that I wanted, but I couldn't even be there for my own family as well. My two boys and husband are the world to me. I thank my Pilates world daily, as I met my soul mate and husband on a blind date set up by my clients who were also his colleagues. He is the most supportive man a wife and mother would want and has always been there to pull me through the hard days—always my biggest cheerleader.

The decision of whether to keep the Pilates studio open or to close it was taking a huge toll on my physical, emotional, and financial well-being. I wanted to be home more with my family, but I couldn't even say the words "close the studio." It was my first baby! Not literally, of course, but the time, energy, and devotion that go into creating your own life through your career is a nurturing endeavor much like motherhood.

I still enjoyed my time with my clients, but I knew with everything in me that this had to stop, change, and evolve. After a series of business and personal hardships, I did not trust those around me. My ego was keeping me small and stuck, and I was not living for my soul's best interest.

The amount of times that I had planned to cut out the parts of my business that left me feeling a lack of abundance were too many to count.

The constant thoughts that flooded my brain day and night were too many to count.

The anxious thoughts of how and when I would tell my clients that there would be no more group classes were too many to count.

When we choose to stay small and stuck, we are not aligning ourselves with our true desires, our highest paths, and we can play that game for only so long.

I received visionary advice from a mind-set coach, and from that I concluded that I had become overwhelmed with thinking that closing the group classes would be abandoning my clients. I felt continually worried that I was leaving my clients, but in truth I was abandoning my own desires and my family. I craved to do more online work to let my creativity shine but felt that would let others down. It didn't seem aligned with my heart to turn away from my brick-and-mortar studio, because I didn't yet know how I would still be able to serve my clients. I felt that keeping the studio was what I was expected to do for others—completely disregarding my own desires.

The last thing I wanted to do was not be there for the clients who had been in my life for so long—some had been along for the ride the entire eleven years. We had been together through all aspects of *life*: births, adoptions, infertility, miscarriages, loss of children, abuse, gender transitioning, empty nests, loss of husbands, cancer,

MS, Parkinson's, strokes, heart disease, addictions, Alzheimer's, affairs, divorces, mental-health issues, suicides, and death.

I had a deep sense of sadness, feeling that I would be turning away from my Pilates family. But in reality I had already abandoned them with my energy and had already been turning away from them during this whole indecisive struggle. I felt a lot of clarity after the session, but as I had so many other times over the last year, I wondered how I would really implement this new level of advice and truly act on it for the good of my family and myself.

I wanted to align with this new peace.

So many business owners have felt that same way. We realize that we sometimes stay with our clients for all the wrong reasons. We spend too much energy feeling obligated to stay with them because we want to stay with our tribe. But if we are constantly trying to stay with our tribe, to stay relatable, then we are not being their leader; we are only being their peer.

Ultimately, we don't grow, because we feel guilty for leaving them and we let fear take over. Fear does not foster growth.

How did I finally implement these changes?

Well, the very next day, I walked into my garage to get a broom and stepped on a garden flat rake (which wasn't put away—I had no idea it was coming), and it clocked me on my head as hard as a baseball bat. Interestingly, the blow to my head was at my left forehead—very close to my third-eye chakra. I got hit in my mind's eye, because it was closed for me. I wasn't paying attention to or able to see what was right in front of me.

A popular Oprah saying really resonates: "The universe will first speak to you in a whisper, and when those whispers don't get your attention, the universe will give you a smack upside the head."

The universe had no choice but to smack me upside the head and get me to actually listen and take action this time. I was forced to cancel the group classes immediately and essentially all the types of sessions that were leaving me feeling small, stuck, and filled with anxiety.

The concussion has proved to be a blessing and has opened me back up to trusting people, the universe, and God. It came as a reminder to reframe the negative as positive. It showed me that I am worth aligning with my desires. I needed the blow to the head to open my life up to miracles, to take the leap and make changes in my business. It has reminded me to deeply feel that things happen *for* us, not *to* us, and to constantly be open to miracles and connections. It allowed me to follow my desire of reaching and serving more women through Pilates and fitness and getting better results by adding mind-set training to those modalities. It has allowed me to help those suffering with brain injuries and chronic pain to reframe the negative as positive and given me more empathy for those walking that path. There are still many lingering symptoms with post-concussion syndrome, but I wouldn't change the course of events given the many *shifts* that have resulted in a more beautifully aligned life. Not only did I *not* abandon my clients, but I created new business streams that serve them more, and I also now get to inspire as many women as possible on a global basis, which was always my desire.

As a result, I now get to enjoy a life with my husband and kids where I get to kiss them before bed every night.

ABOUT LISA KHERA

Lisa Khera is a wife and the mother of two boys; a certified Stott Pilates, BarreConcept, and PiYo instructor; and an author. In 2000, she started taking Pilates mat and reformer classes and instantly realized the many benefits Pilates provides. In 2006, she started her entrepreneurial journey, owning and operating her Pilates studio, In Balance Pilates, in Ottawa, Canada.

Trained in gerontology and as a physiotherapy assistant, she went from having chronic low-back pain to being pain-free and strong with Pilates, fitness, and mind-set work.

Lisa inspires other like-minded women to obtain optimal posture through direct support in person at her studio and online internationally through digital Pilates courses, sessions, and coaching. She has a special interest in applying the Pilates principles to help her clients rehab chronic pain; she enjoys working with clients that have brain injuries and always makes time to help Pilates instructors pass their Pilates exams. She is passionate about helping other entrepreneurs strategize and begin their business ventures. Her ideal day includes the beach, travel, and workouts with her husband and two boys.

Reach Lisa here:

lisa@inbalancepilates.ca

InBalancePilates.ca

Instagram: @lisakhera
Facebook:
In Balance Pilates Studio
Lisa's birth story is featured in the book *Yoga Birth Method*.

Chapter 15

COURAGE AS THE CATALYST FOR PERSONAL TRUTH

I asked several friends what about me inspires them, and the answers were as follows: my kindness, my ability to cultivate fun and laughter, my generosity, my creativity, and then one that surprised me, my courage! As I thought about this, I followed my memories all the way back to first grade, when I was too shy to even answer "here" to roll call. In fact, the perception of shyness is a common memory all through my youth and even into my career as a lawyer. Fast-forward to now, when I aspire to speak on large stages and have a positive impact in the world, and as I speak up for others, I have indeed cultivated courage for myself. My greatest joy is helping others to find their voices and live their greatest truth and purpose. I have learned to do this by first learning to do it for myself.

Back to first grade. I was so quiet I was tested to see whether there was anything "wrong" with me. In the tests they discovered, apparently, that I was very bright, and I was immediately moved to advanced learning groups in school. What these teachers failed to know about me is that I did in fact have inner courage and tenacity; I would simply say no to assignments that made no sense to me and was out on the playground offering bravery lessons (as I remember calling them) to meek friends, as I saw their timid approach to life. I began to find my own strength by being present for others. It is only recently in my life that I have learned that showing up *as myself* requires my greatest courage. Although it is noble and worthy to assist others, I first had to find courage to use my own voice and to live my truth.

I had a rather miserable high-school experience in that my shyness greatly impaired my ability to really engage in life fully. That said, I learned quickly I was a natural champion of the perceived misfits and learned to embrace my introversion. I started to bloom as a senior and took on lifeguarding at a local water park and began to focus on what I really wanted. It was then that I learned to express myself through writing and spent hours visualizing my desires and naturally gravitating to what I now know as meditation. I learned discipline through body building and aerobics and even dabbled in competitions and running events. I discovered that I could will myself into about any position, which resulted in a long series of hard lessons. I ran my way through college and found myself in law school at age twenty. At that time, life seemed like an endless competition, and I engaged in it as such.

The first time I realized that running to get ahead in life was not serving me in the highest way was when I experienced what I would describe as a spiritual opening while in my final year of law school. While I always knew it was important to know what you wanted to do in life, this period showed me something dramatically important to my truth.

Suddenly, when I was only a few weeks from graduating law school but had already been hired by a prestigious law firm located in a downtown Miami skyscraper, I had the strongest sense that in fact law was not enough about helping people. I had a compulsion to volunteer without any agenda besides offering my heart. I would sit on my apartment couch every morning and pray for people who were less fortunate than I perceived myself to be (having a supportive family and the means to help myself into the fast lane of life). I would cry a lot during that time, wondering what the meaning of living truly was. I knew having children and a mortgage and chasing shiny objects was not my purpose, yet that is exactly what ensued in some form, except that I did not have my own children.

Despite a growing awareness of my desire to lead a deeply purposeful life, I took the bar exams and began work at the Miami firm. Something that took even greater courage occurred at that time: I began dating one of my former college professors, who was over twenty years older. I remember the day I took my parents to lunch and shared my news with them. I knew this man would be my husband because I felt deep within my spirit that his wisdom and sharing would be pivotal to my growth as a human being and spiritual being. We married within a year of our first date; this man became my life teacher and mentor.

I lasted less than four months in the Miami law firm. I was bored beyond belief and cried myself to work every day. I knew the work was not my calling, as I found no joy or purpose in it. I sat in a law library, doing legal analysis, when I knew my passion and purpose was to work directly with people in impactful ways. Every day I would literally mark days off my calendar, a bit like Tom Hanks did on the tree in the movie where he was stranded on an island after being lost at sea. I was lost at sea—I had no sense of purpose beyond knowing that my soon-to-be husband had great purpose as part of his life's work and expression. After we married, I had no job for a while—I fell deeper into what felt like a purposeless hole. I would count the days since my graduation as proof to myself that I was still on track—that I had not lost the race to some unknown point of success that I thought life to be. During that time in my life, I hid behind my relationship as proof that I had purpose—his purpose. Of course, this later became another of my greatest moments of courage—that is, to separate from him around the year 2000 and begin my own spiritual journey.

At that time, I began going to personal-growth conferences and workshops on my own. I began taking personal responsibility for my growth and my unhappiness. I started my master's degree in mental-health counseling, dreaming of a day when I could work with people by discussing with them their deepest yearnings and experiences. After all, this was the work I had always longed to do, but when I was choosing a career, with all good intentions, my parents cautioned me that I might not make a good living. I confronted my depression by entering therapy and even took medication to moderate my depression, which had been building since high school. I later learned that depression would manifest anytime I got too far out of alignment with my deepest yearnings and what

I now refer to as my soul's purpose. I also learned that the best antidote to that depression (aside from learning to cultivate my highest truth in living my life) is to travel, be creative, and engage in spiritual teachings.

In the mid-1990s, I opened and ran a satellite office for a large Orlando-based law firm. I practiced in the area of injury law and civil rights, feeling at least I could pour my heart into the work and help people find their voices. Despite finishing my master's degree, I lacked the courage to leave law. I was making a fantastic income and had some sense of security. I later learned that this security was the kind of status quo that leads to stagnation and death of the spirit—I was no longer doing what I wanted to do but rather rationalizing a career track because it afforded me, literally even, the ability to help my family and empower people through money. Once again, that mistake would become one of my many lessons in life: money can never be *the* reason for me, anyway. Still, it was a hard habit to break. I spent my thirties chasing many shiny objects and rationalizing that my income afforded me the opportunity for sacred travel, where I would meet some of the most potent teachers of my life.

Enter the shamans. I attended the International Transpersonal Association Conference in Manaus, Brazil, where I would again experience a huge spiritual opening, awareness, and teachers I continue to work with and learn from to this day. The conference was entitled "Technologies of the Sacred," and one night in the deep jungle of the Amazon, I experienced the power of the sacred plant teacher ayahuasca. It remains one of the most pivotal experiences of my life in that I experienced myself and the world around me with visions of the actual energy of the plants, knowing my true divinity, experiencing telepathy and feelings of bliss and awareness that I had never imagined possible. I have continued working with indigenous traditions and teachers since that time, and it has been another of the greatest gifts of my life.

Fast-forward to the last five years. One of my greatest life challenges occurred in 2012, when I had overstayed my position with the large law firm by so long that I began to make unclear choices and harbored much resentment toward my employers despite the fact that they had nothing to do with my unhappiness. This resulted in a very nasty parting of ways, which threatened my reputation as a lawyer and certainly taught me the error of overstaying anything in life that is not serving my growth or life purpose. I would then make another pivotal decision by continuing to fight for my identity as a practicing lawyer by opening my own firm. In retrospect, it never occurred to me then that stopping *is an action*! As it turns out, I have learned a lot running my own business, especially the value of taking responsibility for everything in my life. I no longer blame anything or anyone for how I feel or for what occurs in life. It may seem particularly ironic given the type of law I practice is generally all about helping clients claim victim status and get money for doing so.

As I write today, I have learned never to force something to fit, whether it be a job, a relationship, or even an opportunity. I now have taken my own despair I felt while practicing law and transmuted it by launching a coaching and consulting platform that helps lawyers and others live life without having to check their souls at the door. I am finally living the truth of who I am: I am a soulful woman who loves and helps with her whole heart, who needs travel and eclectic spiritual deepening from all traditions to feed her soul, and who will never sell out in depletion of her soul's purpose in work or any facet of life.

Blessings on your journey!

ABOUT PAMELA MICHELLE

Pamela Michelle, JD, MS, graduated with honors from the University of Florida (BA, political science) before entering law school at age twenty. Obtaining her juris doctorate in 1991, she was admitted to both the Georgia bar and Florida bar.

Through 1996 she was defense counsel for corporations in injury/litigation and labor/civil-rights cases. For the past twenty-one years, she has served in these same areas as plaintiff's counsel. After working in two large law firms, she opened her own practice in 2012.

Pam obtained her MS in mental-health counseling in 2004 and has completed over one thousand therapy hours assisting clients. Certified as a coach by the International Coaching Federation, she shares her coaching and consulting practice with individuals from all walks of life.

Pam has done intensive study under numerous masters of ancient wisdom, neuroscience, philosophy, world religions, indigenous and sacred traditions, and mindfulness/insight practices. She continues on this path as a lifelong learner, seeker, adviser, and teacher. Incorporating a passion for transpersonal, humanistic, and existential perspectives into her coaching and consulting work, her world view unfolded through extensive travel and a constant quest for self-actualization.

Pam's greatest passion is to help others "deep dive" into their own inner being, allowing the radiant beauty of their soul's purpose to emerge forth into the world, resulting in self-fulfillment and a calming sense of wholeness. The goal is to achieve a profound alchemical transformation of consciousness.

As the founder and CEO of SoulofLawyers.com, the Soul of Lawyers Network, and PamelaMichelle.com, Pam offers platforms for coaching, consulting, speaking, sacred travel, and networking opportunities.

Pam can be contacted at Pam@pamelamichelle.com or Pam@ souloflawyers.com.

Chapter 16

THE WAKE-UP CALL

As I sat with my husband in the cold, sterile conference room, waiting to get the results, tensions were high. It was the day we had been dreading for the past few months. I knew in my gut that something wasn't right with our two-and-a-half-year-old son, but today was the day when we were finally to receive an official diagnosis.

As much as I was dreading it, I was praying that we would finally have answers and a solution.

But what happened next gave us little hope.

It was as if I was having an out-of-body experience when I heard the news delivered that my son, Beckett, was autistic. I can't remember the exact words spoken, but it was said so casually. It was as if someone had dropped a bomb in my lap and then acted as though it weren't a big deal. It might explode; it might not. We don't know.

My husband, Jason, asked whether our son would ever be able to function normally or attend a regular school.

They had no answers. There was no protocol.

The only advice given was to get him in day care around other kids for *socialization* and to enroll him in speech therapy, but there were no guarantees. There wasn't a medication they could prescribe or anything specific we could do to help him get better.

I couldn't believe what was happening. We had just been slapped with the life-altering news that our son was autistic and may never lead a *normal* life, and it felt as if we had just gotten a greeting card that said, "Hey, here's a pile of crap. Good luck with that."

I spent the first few months after his diagnosis feeling sorry for myself. I remember the despair and hopelessness and then the guilt I felt for thinking, "Why me, God?" I was so pissed at God. I thought, "Why would you do this to me?" I had already been through so many struggles. This happened to other people. This wasn't supposed to happen to me.

I had come from nothing. I was born to teenage parents and grew up in poverty with a very unstable home. But despite where I started, I was determined to make something of myself. I was determined to beat the odds and become financially successful and have a happy marriage and family life. I wanted to give my kids all the things that I never had: stability, love, and most importantly, opportunities for a better life.

In the first five years of marriage, we had managed to survive a bankruptcy and almost getting divorced not once or twice but three times. Coming from a broken home with stepparents coming in and out of my life like a revolving door, I was determined to break that family cycle.

It took a lot of work and a few come-to-Jesus moments—literally. But we managed to make it through stronger. So when this happened, it was a total WTF moment. Like, are you kidding me right now? Things were finally good in my world, for once in my life, and now I was facing a huge obstacle with my child that I felt powerless to do anything about.

On the outside looking in, we were the perfect all-American family. Just like the Jeffersons, we had upgraded from the trailer park to a really nice home on the East Side. My husband and I were both fulfilling our passions as entrepreneurs. We were like local celebrities and knew everyone in the small town that we lived in. We couldn't even go grocery shopping without someone stopping us.

We were finally on the path to success, and things seemed really good.

I was so focused on my career and proving not only to others but also to myself that I was completely oblivious to what was going on around me. I mean, yeah, I would ask the pediatrician at every appointment why my son wasn't speaking yet and whether I should be concerned, but it was always brushed off. "You're just comparing him to your daughter," he would say. "Boys don't develop as quickly as girls."

And I didn't question it. Why would I? Medical doctors were just one degree below Jesus himself, and you never, I mean never, question a doctor's authority.

The same month that Beckett went in for his testing, I hit the highest rank in my direct-sales company. This is embarrassing to admit, but for the first time in my life, I finally felt important. It didn't matter how I had grown up, because I was proving that I was worthy and capable of creating what looked like success.

And then we got the diagnosis, and the rug was pulled out from under me. It was like no, you can't have that success. That success is not for you. And so my business began to crumble around me. Heck, my *life* came crashing down all around me. And before I could even begin to focus on him, I had to hit rock bottom. And boy, did I ever.

It was the big wake-up call that I had no idea I was waiting on.

It was during the aftermath that I realized just how bad my own health situation had become.

I was addicted to prescription drugs. I took something to wake up, to go to sleep, for depression, for anxiety, and to focus, and then something to counteract all the side effects.

I was dealing with crippling panic attacks, extreme fatigue, joint pain, migraines, and just a general feeling of suckiness. My energy levels had fallen so low that the only way I could get any work done was to double and sometimes triple my dose of Adderall.

Looking back, I have no idea how I survived.

It wasn't until Jason stepped in and said, "Brooke, what the hell are you doing? You're thirty years old, and you're killing yourself!" that I woke up.

When I came off my medications, it was as if a veil had been lifted. The fog that had been hanging over me finally dissipated, and I could actually think for myself again.

When I saw how much medical intervention had been hurting me, it was the catalyst that helped me switch from a place of despair to a place of "I can do something about this." If I could overcome all the other devastating things that had happened in my life, then I could empower myself through this situation with my child.

He was counting on me because no one else was going to be an advocate for him. No one else gave us any hope. I was encouraged to join support groups for parents affected by autism, and I refused. To me, that meant giving up and *coping*. My son deserved better than that.

I refused to accept that he wouldn't be able to communicate to tell me that he loved me or tell me about his day. I refused to be OK with the meltdowns, the sleep issues, and the poop smearing. I refused to live my life in constant fear that he would disappear in a crowded area. I refused to believe that there was nothing I could do about it, so I strapped on my invisible superhero cape and got busy researching.

We didn't have the money to do any of the fancy therapies that I read about online, but we had to eat anyhow, so I started there. Everything that I read led me back to diet and toxins going into our bodies. The more I learned, the angrier I got at the medical establishment and our government. The vaccines, the medications I was told were safe during pregnancy, the endless rounds of antibiotics—I began questioning everything. I was like, well, they lied about this, so what else are they lying about? So the rabbit hole got deeper and deeper.

I was struggling to stay in a positive frame of mind, managing my new life as the mom to an autistic child, when a friend of mine suggested that I check out a movie called *The Secret*. That was when I went from "Maybe I can make a difference" to "I'm going to see whether this law of attraction stuff really works." So I decided to put it to the ultimate test and heal my son from autism. Keep in mind that we were told up front that there is *no cure.*

I made my vision board and placed a photo of my son on it with the words "Thank you for Beckett's healing. Beckett is healed." I began praying over him at night, asking for his healing and thanking God as if it had already happened. I continued to research and learn what I could about how certain foods could affect his health and behavior.

But I had no idea that making healthy lifestyle changes would affect every aspect of our lives. I became that mom with a stick up her butt, analyzing labels, being the ingredient detective. Let me see the label. What's in it? No, he can't have that. Well, can he have this? No, he can't have that either. It resulted in us taking our own food almost everywhere we went, spending hours in the grocery store reading labels, and feeling like social outcasts who could no longer enjoy a simple birthday party without special arrangements. It made me realize how everything we do as a culture is centered around eating unhealthy food.

I was often met with eye rolls and people who couldn't understand why he couldn't have just a little gluten. Everything about my life felt so serious, so restricted, and so difficult. We began passing up invitations, and then people just stopped inviting us.

Those three years were some of the hardest and loneliest of my life.

Not only did I feel isolated from how everyone in the rest of the world was living, but I had to begin standing up for myself and my child in ways that I had never had the guts to do before.

I had enough of being berated and demonized by doctors for choosing to forgo additional vaccinations. It wasn't just the doctors.

It was the nurses, the school officials, day care staff, family, friends, everyone. I was even snubbed by a lady who had cared for my son in the church nursery because we had declined the flu vaccine.

I didn't know for sure whether vaccines had anything to do with his diagnosis, but I knew that there was enough doubt in my mind that I had to follow my instincts and say no until I knew more. Here I was, trying to protect my child as best as I could from further damage, and I was being treated as if I were abusing him.

My instincts were justified because the more we moved away from the medical establishment as a whole and the more he ate fresh fruits and vegetables and real food, the more Beckett's health began to improve. We started implementing more natural healing methods and went to the doctor only when it was an absolute emergency.

Right before his fifth birthday, he finally began speaking in sentences. Every day we would ask him, "Beckett, what did you do at school today?" and he would only grunt. Then he would say yes as if to acknowledge that he went to school. I'll never forget when he came home from day care and proudly announced that he had watched a movie that day. It was a huge turning point in our journey and exactly what we needed to know that we were doing the right thing.

I had started standing in my power, listening to my instincts, and doing what was best for my son, despite what society told me. It was so incredibly difficult because I was being judged at every move. All the professionals were scoffing at us. We didn't have support from family. But we knew we were doing the best that we could for our son. We were fighting to give him a chance in life, and it was finally paying off.

As much as I resisted going into a doctor's office, Beckett was required to get a checkup for school, so I begrudgingly scheduled an appointment. We waited for months to be able to see a doctor who was known for being lenient on parents who chose not to vaccinate. He came in and assessed my son. He looked over Beckett's chart repeatedly and said, "I don't see any signs of autism."

He went on to say that based on what was in those records, he was expecting a completely different child.

He was amazed. He asked us what we were doing, and when we told him, he applauded us. It was the first time that a medical doctor or professional had ever given us any praise. He told us to keep doing what we were doing because it was clearly working and then went on to tell us that he was dropping the autism diagnosis from his medical chart.

We were overjoyed. And more importantly, I was validated. Finally. After all the hard work, someone who had the credentials was saying, yes, this was working. I was so excited to share Beckett's story. I just knew that it was going to inspire so many people. I could not believe that it had actually worked and he was healed.

So I went out, and I started yelling it from the rooftops. I was so proud, and more importantly, I knew that if only people could hear our story, they would find hope. But what I found was that not everyone was happy for us.

Some people nitpicked, telling me, "You can't use the word 'healed.' You have to use the word 'recovery.'" But he *was* healed; he was cured. Some people called me a liar outright. Some questioned his diagnosis. Some told me that he was still autistic and we were just masking his symptoms. Some told me they were happy for me but weren't going to share the story with people they knew facing the same thing, because they didn't want to give them false hope. Some called me irresponsible for sharing his story.

At first, I didn't understand. I was so crushed. Why were people pissing on our success? Why were people who didn't know my son and who had never seen his medical records telling me what he did or didn't have? Why were they telling me what I could and couldn't say?

I've never once heard someone say that he or she beat cancer only to have another person call him or her a liar because someone else the other person knew died from it.

It was so upsetting that I stopped openly sharing his recovery story. It became sacred. It wasn't up for debate. It was my story. It was my truth. I had lived through the hell and come out victorious on the other side. Why couldn't I share it without being attacked?

While my son's autism diagnosis was one of the most devastating events in my life, it was also the most important because it was my wake-up call.

Not only was I able to heal my son, but I was able to heal myself with proper nutrition. There's no telling where I would be right now without having been nudged in that direction with his diagnosis.

It taught me finally to stand up for myself and speak up when I didn't agree with something. When I was growing up in the South, women didn't speak for themselves or make waves, so standing up to authority figures was a big deal.

I learned to listen to my intuition and trust my instincts— something that I wasn't capable of doing when I was so highly medicated. By the way, I was divinely guided through this process and would never claim to be able to help someone else with recovery. I can only share our story and what worked for us.

It taught me that people do not like their belief systems to be questioned, because if I'm right, if what I'm saying is true, then it makes them feel that what they believe is wrong. Therefore, they're not open even to hearing Beckett's story, because they already believe autism cannot be cured. I also learned that it's not about me; it's simply a reflection of their beliefs being projected onto me, oftentimes in anger.

I truly believe that my mind-set and inability to give up despite the challenges we faced were crucial to his success. I believed that he could and would be cured, that he would be healed, that miracles can happen, that God Almighty still has the power to deliver us from darkness.

As an entrepreneur and someone with larger-than-life goals, I was prepared for the harsh reality that not everyone will be happy for your success. Not everyone will applaud you when you climb the mountain. There will be haters and naysayers.

I learned that if you want extraordinary results, don't follow societal norms.

This experience unlocked something within me that I didn't know existed. It unleashed the lioness, the protector, and the woman who is unstoppable even when backed against a wall. Most importantly, I learned that I am capable of anything.

ABOUT BROOKE RASH

Brooke Rash is a serial entrepreneur and social-media addict who turned her obsession into a career. She first began growing her social-media presence as she took her followers on her son's autism-recovery journey. Brooke now helps others position their stories to monetize their businesses through social media. In 2016, she and her husband, Jason, used their social-marketing skills to help their entrepreneur friends generate more than a half million dollars in revenue. That inspired her to create The Social Celebrity, a brand that highlights A-list entrepreneurs. Brooke believes that social media is a powerful platform, and by creating influence, you can use it to cash in on your star power.

Website: www.TheSocialCelebrity.com

Facebook: https://www.facebook.com/brooke.rash.9

Chapter 17

A JOURNEY TO FIND PEACE

I was always an anxious child. I began to notice it somewhere around the age of nine. My grandfather was dying, and my mother was one of his caretakers. I was often with her. I remember waking up in the middle of the night not being able to breathe. My parents took me to the doctor, who diagnosed it as anxiety. Even at a young age, you are affected by what you are around and don't even know it.

During my childhood I was anxious, not knowing what it was. I had constant stomach aches, so much so that in high school I pretty much stopped eating. I graduated at my lowest weight of 105 pounds. Anxiety can take such a toll on your body.

I always had insecurities. I never felt pretty enough, skinny enough, popular enough. I am not really sure where all the insecurities came from. I had a fantastic, supportive family. These insecurities are what led to future events in my life.

After graduating high school, I went to cosmetology school. I loved it! I felt as though I had finally found my calling. And it was so different from high school. I made new friends, and we were all on the same level. No popularity contests.

I met a guy soon after and loved all his friends, going out all the time, and really having fun! I thought I was finally figuring my life out. As time went on, our relationship developed, and so did the jealousy. He was constantly torturing me over old boyfriends and even over my friends who were girls. Because of this I totally stopped my old life. I had hardly any contact with my old friends. I even distanced myself a bit from my family.

The mental abuse from jealousy developed into physical abuse. First it was just a push. I remember falling down from a push and jamming my finger pretty badly. It was huge and black and blue. I covered it up when asked what happened. I said I fell and jammed it. The fighting got more intense. Two times that I remember, I was dropped off in the middle of the night on dark roads by myself. I got out of the car so that he would not slam my head into the window again. One of the times, I was on a dark highway all alone. I walked to a truck stop that wasn't very far away. I was shaking, crying, and scared to death. While I was walking, I thought, "Who am I going to call to come get me?" I couldn't tell anyone that I was putting up with this! I knew it was wrong, but he had convinced me that somehow this was my fault. That night, before I could contact help, he came back and picked me up.

Even after this, I stayed. I was too embarrassed to tell anyone. Fight after fight, I stayed. If I even looked in the path of another guy, a fight would start with the nasty name-calling.

I went to a wedding with a huge rug burn on my head from being pushed into the carpet and dragged along it. I told everyone I burnt my head with a curling iron. Deep down inside, I was begging for someone to know the truth and come save me. I didn't see at the time that I was the only one who could save me. During one of the worst fights, I was kicked in the crotch and told, "I hope your children are born with something wrong with them someday." Yes, you read that right! Then came the final straw. I was pushed down into the carpet and had something held to my head that felt like a gun. I didn't see it, and to this day I am not sure whether it was a gun. In the moment, I just begged to live and for him to leave me alone.

I was miserable and scared to tell anybody. I remember calling an old friend a few times and wanting to scream, "Come and get me!" I was hoping my friend could read my mind. But I just hung up when my friend answered. I was too embarrassed. I was too scared of what would happen if he found out I called somebody.

Finally I got the courage to get out of the relationship! I did. I was free. Thank God I was free! I was sad, scared, and so happy, all at the same time.

I never told anyone about the abuse. I buried it deep down inside as if it never happened. It was over; why did I need to talk about it? Burying something like this seems so easy, but it does come back eventually.

I started living as if none of this had ever happened. I eventually met my husband. He was and is the complete opposite of whom I was with before. He is so kindhearted, loving, and not jealous or possessive.

We got married and some years later decided we wanted to have children. Having a child did not turn out to be as easy as I thought it was going to be. I thought that as a woman, I would just get pregnant—that is what a woman's body does. But it wasn't that easy for me. I started obsessing about it. I thought this was something I should be able to control. How could this be happening?

After close to seven years, we had our baby girl. It took years of IUI after IUI, and we did not have any results. During shot after shot in my legs and my stomach, I would think, "OK, this is the time. I have a good feeling; it is going to happen." It was always followed by disappointment. I finally went to a new doctor and had my first session of in vitro fertilization. I did get pregnant but miscarried right away. I had two rounds of methotrexate for my body to expel the fetus from my body. Because of those shots, I had to wait six months to try again. Round two, I got pregnant. It finally happened April 15, 2009. We had our beautiful baby girl.

I wasn't very anxious at first when we brought her home. I actually felt relaxed being home with her, until she got very sick after her first birthday. The anxiety started to set in! I began having a fear of germs, which developed into a fear of bringing her anywhere. I did not want her to be around people. I was a mess. I started losing weight, not sleeping, and worrying twenty-four hours a day.

My mom begged me to see a doctor, which I did, and I was diagnosed with anxiety. I was put on medication to help control the anxiety. As time went on and I sheltered my daughter, I started to feel a bit better. My husband and I decided we wanted our daughter to have a sibling. I had gone off the anxiety medicine months before. We tried to get pregnant on our own, but again it was not happening. I had embryos frozen from my round of in vitro when I had my daughter. I told myself that if it was meant to be, it would happen. We were having only one embryo implanted. We knew the odds were not very good, between my age and our implanting only one embryo. We knew we could not go through the months and years of doctors and treatments to get pregnant again. We prayed, "Dear God, if this is meant to be, let it happen. If not, we understand, and we have a beautiful healthy daughter already."

Well, it was meant to be! I was pregnant with a baby boy. I had a decent pregnancy until a scan showed that my umbilical cord was missing a vessel that carried blood and oxygen to the baby. I was so afraid something was going to be wrong with the baby. But he was born perfectly healthy on December 7, 2012.

I remember being in the hospital and not feeling the happiness I had felt when I had my daughter. I felt depressed and worried, not happy. We came home from the hospital, and I cried twenty-four hours a day. No one knew except my immediate family and a close friend whom I cried on the phone to. I remember calling a doctor's office to set up a test for my son, and I cried so much on the phone with the receptionist that she called me back later that day to see whether I was OK.

I had postpartum depression. How could this have happened? I had everything I wanted in life—two beautiful, healthy children; a loving, supportive husband; and a beautiful house. "What is wrong with me?" I would think. But I could not control the depression and crying.

I saw a doctor after thinking awhile it would just go away. I was put on an antidepressant again. I eventually started feeling better—not crying as much, not worrying as much. So after about a year or so of being on the medication, I stopped taking it.

I was good for about six months. Little did I know it was all going to come crashing down around me when my son got sick with a stomach bug. He was two years old and ended up in the ER because he was so sick. The rest of us got it too, which caused us not to have Easter dinner at our house as planned or my daughter's birthday party. These are minor things, I know, but this rocked my world and put me in a tailspin.

The germophobia set in again. The constant scary thoughts going through my head started again. I was scared to go anywhere, especially with my children. I started to become very physically sick. I was constantly sick to my stomach with fear. I had a constant rapid heartbeat and always felt dizzy. It got so bad that I would vomit and feel as if I was going to pass out. It wasn't until my hands went numb during one of these episodes that I realized I was having panic attacks. I then started having fear of panic attacks. I left work in the middle of doing someone's hair because I was so sick to my stomach I swore I was getting a stomach virus. It was another panic attack. After the panic attack, I would be wiped out for a day.

My germophobia got worse. Way worse. I refused to bring my kids to public places, and if for some reason we were in one, I would make them wash their hands constantly. I would not touch doorknobs anywhere. I would actually wait until another person was going to a door in a public place and let the person open it. I would use my elbows on doors so I didn't have to touch them with my hands.

I was so sick that I lost a ton of weight and started again not to go anywhere. I was getting so depressed. I didn't want to live like this. The feeling of fear inside of you twenty-four hours a day is horrific. I wanted to run away. I felt that my children and husband would be better off without my constant worry and fear. I felt I was ruining my children and my marriage. Honestly, I had those quick moments of not wanting to live. That is how depressed I was. Thankfully, I knew deep down that would not help anybody.

One day I woke up and said, "I cannot live like this for another minute. I am not living life. I am fearing it." I contacted some coaches to help me with my anxiety and fears, and I saw a psychologist.

With the help of all these wonderful people and a lot of books, I learned where a lot of this anxiety was coming from—it was my need to be in control. But I was not in control. My life was actually out of control. Years before, I had made a mental note that I would always have control of my life. Nothing and no one would hurt my family or me. I needed to control where my children were so that they did not get sick. I had to be in control, and when I was not in control, I was in so much fear that I made myself mentally and physically sick.

People think having anxiety and depression is a choice. It is not a choice—it is an illness. People do not want to lose friends, constantly cry, not go places, silently weep, hope not to wake up, and have the feeling of wanting it all just to end—and then wake up and do it all over again. You cannot "just get over it." Depression and anxiety is an illness, not a choice.

I have learned to actually welcome anxiety. I have made peace with it. I talk to it and ask, "What are you trying to tell me?" I also write about it. I journal almost every day. The good and the bad, I write it all down. I have learned to laugh! I did not laugh for a very long time! Just smiling can put you in a better mood. I have learned to love more. I have learned to meditate and use EFT tapping. I also use deep breathing and mindfulness. I have realized that I am enough. I have realized that I have gone through this to help others. I have always wanted to help, and have often helped, others going through anxiety and panic attacks. That is the gift that I have received from anxiety: the gift of realizing my own power, not the power that it had over me.

I realized I am a survivor!

ABOUT MANDY SCANLON

Mandy Scanlon has been a professional stylist for over 10 years. She has always had a passion for beauty and making people feel beautiful from the inside out.

She is a certified Ignitor Coach™ in coaching for self-esteem, anxiety, panic attacks, and feeling your best in your own skin.

She is married to the love of her life, Pat, and has two children, Lila and Finn. She loves the beach and sunshine!

Mandy's unique business is to help men and women feel more confident in their own skin and learn how to dress to feel confident, along with coaching for anxiety, depression, panic, and negative thinking.

She can be contacted at mandyscanlon.com. She offers unique courses in the following:

- Boosting self-esteem and body image
- Coaching for positive thinking and confidence
- Style color and wardrobe confidence
- Overcoming unhappiness and depression
- Changing self-limiting beliefs

Mandy would love to hear from you!

Chapter 18

OLD GREMLIN, NEW TRICKS

We all start off as perfect little humans, with no hang-ups about ourselves. Studies show that the only two fears we are born with are the fear of falling and the fear of loud noises. Everything else—from the fear of failing to the fear of the creepy old man down the street who dresses up as a scarecrow on Halloween—is a learned fear.

We learn to fear by directly experiencing something ourselves or by being taught by others. Rationally speaking, if we learn something, we should be able to unlearn it. However, thanks to evolution, our brains work to preserve us. That means that our fears and other negative thoughts get much more airtime in our subconscious than the positive thoughts do. That is a fantastic quality for keeping safe from saber-toothed tigers but not so much when we are doing something as benign as interviewing for a job.

Our fears can impact our lives to varying degrees. However, it is oftentimes the fears we create ourselves that have the most influence. And the fears and doubts about our own self-worth—whether conscious or subconscious—are the most powerful of all.

These fears feed on, and are encouraged by, our gremlins. We all have gremlins. They are the voices that tell us we are not good enough and the proof that our inner critics use to show us that we will not succeed. Gremlins are the things in our lives we would rather not think about. Gremlins are our embarrassments, our secret beliefs about ourselves, and the memories that do not serve us but that we can't seem to forget.

Our gremlins make us afraid. They keep us immobile and unassuming. They tell us to settle. They keep us small.

Mine told me I was garbage and took root when I was a young child.

Most people live for Fridays. Growing up, I used to dread them. Half of them, anyhow. Every other weekend, a court order had me leave my mom to go to my dad's house and stay with him (and later with his new family). I hated it. I believe they hated me. Granted, everything I experienced was through the lens of a little girl, so I cannot be certain of motivations or reasons. But, as I've learned since becoming a mom myself, the best way to hurt a mother is to hurt her daughter.

I remember crying for days before those Fridays approached, hitting my head on the walls and stairs, sobbing myself to sleep as my mom held me because I did not want to go. I remember the Polish lullabies she sang to me to calm me down. My mom fought to keep me. She went to court, the police, the hospital, and child-protective services. Some people helped us outside of the system, but no one stopped it. We were alone.

Eventually I learned how to numb my emotions, how to people-please, and how to be invisible. But worst of all, what I learned was that I was powerless. My wants and needs didn't matter. I was nothing.

Growing up thinking you are worthless does not exactly set you on track to be successful. Yes, you absolutely can achieve great things. I was a straight-A student, was a graduate of the US Military Academy at West Point, and had a successful career in the Army for over fourteen years. But my lack of self-worth and my fear that other people would find out I was a fraud were always present, and inside I felt I did not matter.

My fear and sense of unworthiness manifested itself in different ways. I put my own needs last. To be honest, I didn't even know what my true needs and desires were. In relationships and with my career, I was more like a piece of drifting flotsam than an active participant.

I was happy*ish*. Granted, I was secure in my job, I got to go on vacations, and I had friends and family whom I loved. But there was a part of me that was miserable, stressed, and missing that *something*. That is what happens when fear is driving the train—your gremlins take control.

For most of my life, my values and desires were fear based instead of consciousness based. So although I was achieving many great things, I wasn't able to feel true satisfaction. I was always on the lookout for something bad to happen and for my gremlins to pop up.

No matter how hard we try, we cannot make our gremlins go away. They are a part of us. You might be thinking, "Thanks for nothing, Jewell." But before you skip ahead to the next chapter, hear me out. Although you cannot get rid of your gremlins, you can decide how much and what kind of power you give them.

The secret is in the Truth. The gremlins have power because we feed them. Your truth is the story you tell yourself. This story is based on your past experiences, your assumptions, and your interpretations, but it is not necessarily *the* Truth.

For example, I was lucky enough to have my truth turned on its head at two key points in my life. The first time was when my daughter was born and I decided to leave active duty for a life that was aligned with my innermost desires.

The second time was when I almost missed out on becoming a coach because of the truth I was telling myself. I nearly opted out of a high-end self-development program and retreat that I truly wanted to attend, just because I didn't believe in my own worthiness. I had already failed at two businesses and was telling myself that the program wouldn't make a difference for me. So I made up excuses about the investment, the time commitment, and the fact that I was nursing my daughter. But I could not let that nagging feeling in my stomach go. Eventually I decided to attend because I thought the skills I would learn would help me to be a better mom. I enjoyed the program and learned a lot about myself, but it wasn't until the end of the training that I found the courage to set aside my gremlins and jump into the experience full on. The point when I truly committed to thinking differently—when I *allowed* the transformation to occur—my life changed. I learned that my truths of "I am not good enough to do this work" and "I am going to be stuck working jobs that do not give me the fulfillment or freedom I want in order to make a living" weren't the Truth.

So if your truth is not necessarily the Truth, how do you tell the difference and let go of the things that aren't serving you?

The first step is to recognize that your gremlins are the ones directing your decisions. Maybe you are feeling apathetic about your current situation or your future, or you are feeling resistance about something you know you want to do.

Once you are aware of what is going on inside, question it with the tenacity of a six-year-old wanting to know where babies come from. Ask yourself about the things you are feeling, where they came from, and how you know—without a shadow of a doubt—whether they are actually true. I find it helpful to write the answers in a journal (either pen to paper or on the computer). Here are some of my favorites:

- What is the thought I am telling myself?
- Where did that thought come from?
- How can I be absolutely sure that it is true?
- Is there another way to look at this that could also be true?

Most of the time, answering those questions will show you that there is another way to think about the story you are telling yourself, and your truth is not necessarily the Truth.

Next, you reframe your experiences and retask your gremlins. Earlier I said we can't make them go away. But we can change the way we think about them and the way we allow them to affect us. To do that, first sit with them for a while and acknowledge them without judging. Take whatever time you need to heal and forgive. Then ask yourself what you would rather be feeling and what your ideal outcome would look like.

Instead of thinking of your past setbacks and less-than-ideal parts of yourself as purely negative, look at how they have served you. How have they helped you get through difficult situations? How have they taught you to be a wiser, more compassionate, or even more appreciative person? I believe that in just about every hardship, there is something positive from which we can grow. Reframing your perspective, although it seems simple, is an extremely effective way to heal and forgive the past and become more confident in your worth.

As far as the gremlin goes, I recommend giving her a new job. Even though she often keeps you small, she is only trying to keep you safe. Decide what would be a more helpful way for her to do that. Instead of "You are going to fail anyhow, so you might as well just snuggle up with a package of Oreos and binge-watch Netflix," you could ask her to tell you, "You have accomplished so much in your life, and you are going to nail this too." (Just FYI, mine tells me, "You're Jewell F——ing Siebert!")

To be honest, once you reframe and retask, life is not magically going to become all rainbows and unicorns in an instant. There will still be challenges. You'll need to do maintenance work to make sure your mind-set is operating at a positive level. But I know from experience that once you implement these tools, life becomes a million times better. I do not let fear drive the train anymore. I am in touch with my desires; I ask for what I want, and I finally feel free. And anyone can have the same for themselves.

ABOUT JEWELL SIEBERT

Jewell Siebert is an international number one best-selling author and speaker who specializes in productivity and positive mind-set. She has been featured on *Hollywood Live with Jack Canfield*, Bravo, A&E, and the *Huffington Post*. Jewell is the founder of Life Upgraded, a community that helps women enjoy the lives they work so hard to create.

Jewell spent fourteen years on active duty in the US Army and is currently a lieutenant colonel in the Army Reserves. In her coaching practice, Jewell uses her real-world experiences to help her clients find fulfillment, success, and joy. Jewell is also the coauthor of the best-selling books *The Road to Success, Vol. 1, Success University for Women in Business* and *Dear Limits, Get out of My Way!*

In her coaching practice, Jewell uses a combination of mind-set and energy tools along with practical strategies to help her clients create lives that bring them meaning and happiness. She does this through one-on-one coaching, group coaching, live workshops, luxury retreats, and online programs.

Jewell is a graduate of the US Military Academy at West Point, where she majored in Russian and Spanish and minored in environmental engineering. She received her master's in international relations from Saint Mary's University in San Antonio, Texas. Jewell is a certified professional coach (CPC), an energy leadership index master practitioner (ELI-MP), a certified Ignitor Coach™, and a certified Canfield Success Principles Trainer.

To learn more about how you can connect and work with Jewell, please visit her website at JewellSiebert.com, where you can find free resources and information about her programs.

Facebook: @jewellsiebertcoach

Instagram: @jewell.siebert

Twitter: @jewell_siebert

Chapter 19

THIS IS MY NEXT

Remember that not getting what you want is sometimes a wonderful stroke of luck.

—Fourteenth Dalai Lama

My journey of self-awareness started about ten years ago, when I was in my midforties. I started reading many books on self-awareness and ways to be more present in my life. I attended seminars, workshops, and conferences and met wonderful people who helped me become more open-minded to the amazing things that can happen when you allow synchronicity into your life. I was very happy with my journey and thought I had tackled the inner critic that sits in my head. However, after being turned down for a promotion that I was really hoping to get, I turned to the universe and said, "Next." Not getting that job turned out to be the best thing that ever happened to me. But what

I was unprepared for was that my next was going to be one of the biggest challenges ever in my life.

I loved my school. I never dreamed of being a teacher, but when I moved to a small town in Northern Ontario, Canada, I decided to enter teaching and was fortunate to get a job at the school in my new town. I started my career teaching junior kindergarten and then moved to a junior grade, where I stayed for most of my career. During this time, I aspired to enter leadership by being the teacher in charge and taking my principal qualifications. I cannot believe how quickly time has passed since the first day I entered that school. I have grown close to a number of colleagues, and we have seen one another marry, raise our children, separate, divorce, and move to different schools and different positions. Throughout most of my time during my career, I had a vision of myself being a principal. When the time was right, I could see myself leading the teachers and students and leaving a legacy.

When the position became available, I immediately started with my affirmations and a vision board with me as the principal of the school the following year. I worked on my portfolio and worked very hard on cultivating the necessary relationships with parents, knowing that these relationships would serve me in the future. I read and studied in preparation for the interview and handed in what I thought was the best entry plan for that school. Then close to the time of the interview, fear took over, and a limiting belief set in. I stopped believing that I was capable of doing the job. I experienced many feelings of self-doubt.

After what seemed like an eternity after the interview, the day came when I got the phone call letting me know that I was not a successful candidate. I hung up the phone and reflected. I had had a feeling that I would not be a successful candidate, but because of the work I had been doing on self-awareness, I immediately said, "Next." I knew that something just as good or better would come along, and I needed to be open to what the universe had in store for me. But I was not sure what my next was meant to be. I had really hoped that I would be the successful candidate. I asked myself, "Did my limiting belief interfere with the vibration to get the job, or did the universe have other plans for me?"

Over the next year, I continued to work in the same capacity, helping teachers with special-needs students. I also worked at my wellness center by presenting workshops on self-awareness and did some writing.

During the spring, my ninety-two-year-old mother was brought to the hospital and was given a couple of days to live. I was able to take time from work and get to the hospital in time to spend the last few days of her life with her. We shared beautiful moments together, the best ever. We laughed and chatted, and she told me she wasn't ready to go yet, but I knew it was her time and told her that everything would be all right. I was with her when she took her last breath. I was stroking her hair and knew the moment she was gone when the statue she was clutching fell out of her hand.

After her death, when I was looking at family pictures, I came to the realization that my mother never knew how to really love herself. Her husband, my father, had died fifty years ago, and she never fell in love again. She dropped out of life and turned to alcohol to numb her pain. I know she did the best she could. However, her life was full of fear, and those fears and lack of self-love were passed down to me. Suddenly, there was an opening in my heart that I never felt before. I realized that I needed to learn how to love myself and push past fears. Although I had been on my journey of self-awareness for the past ten years, there was still something missing, but I didn't know what it was. The journey to my heart and loving myself was missing, but I was unsure how to begin that journey, so I didn't.

At the end of that school year, I was reassigned to a classroom. Even though I was content in my current position, I knew immediately in my heart that this was where I needed to go. I didn't know why, but I heard the universe calling that this was my next. I knew it would be hard work going back into a classroom, but what I didn't realize was that the hard work would be the inner work that I needed to do on myself. Turns out that I had unfinished life lessons that needed to be completed and new life lessons that the universe was trying to teach me.

It was not until six weeks into the year that the first one reared its ugly head in the form of perfectionism. After working for about six weeks straight, ten hours a day, and things not going as well as I would have liked, I came home and cried. Not really understanding what my pain was about, I had the good fortune to be living with an energy healer. She held me and asked me what my inner child was feeling. I realized that my inner child was furious that I had reverted to my old habits of workaholism and my inner child wanted nothing to do with working ten-hour days. I needed to reflect on what my inner child was saying to me. But where to start?

It became very clear to me that if I had been given the promotion, I may not have been open to my lesson of workaholism. Since I was open to the universe, I realized that the lessons were beginning. I knew that I had to work on ways of self-love. I began to do some mirror work, and as I gazed into the mirror and tried to say the words, "Margaret, I love you," I quickly came to the realization that I was using my name from when I was fourteen years old. And then it hit me: that was when I had changed my name to Maggie from Margaret, and that was when I had begun my journey of self-sabotage behaviors to resist the pain of the emotional traumas that I experienced as a young child. These destructive behaviors continued into my early twenties and then switched to workaholism.

I have been a workaholic for thirty years. I have avoided feeling by keeping busy at something—hours at my job, extra jobs, taking on too many tasks, too many committees, too many commitments, just busy being busy. There is not a moment in the day when I am not busy doing something. Even though I had been on an awakening journey for the past ten years, I was not fully awake. Even though I had done work on the mind by reading and journaling and some meditating, I realized that I was missing something and that I was not fully awake. I came to the realization that I was missing working on my heart. It is a long journey from your head to your heart, and by awakening my inner child, I heard her cries for me to show her more loving-kindness. With this realization, I am now working on giving myself permission to have a healthy combination of work, rest, exercise, and play. Your inner child needs to be empowered with a voice that wants to be heard. This inner child will give you the power to speak with authenticity. Often your inner child has needs that were not met when you were young. If your younger you has experienced emotional, physical, or sexual abuse and if these issues are not resolved, it is difficult to fully live your life as an awakened, authentic person.

Since this awakening, I have become open to the daily lessons that the universe continues to present to me. I am so happy and grateful that I was awake to see that the universe had other plans for me. I believe that my limiting belief of self-doubt and the universe conspired so that I would not get the promotion. Thankfully, I was awake to the universe sending me back into that classroom to tell me that I had unfinished life lessons that needed to be resolved and life lessons that still needed to be learned. My next was the journey I needed to make to awaken my heart more fully and believe in myself. My next is leading me to be the most authentic person that I can be. I encourage you to be open to what the universe is saying and the lessons the universe has to offer. If you or anyone you know has experienced any form of emotional trauma, try some of the following suggestions, which have helped me with my journey from my head to my heart.

1. Begin your day with an hour dedicated to you. Include in your morning routine a combination of journaling, reading, and meditating. Self-awareness expands through your dedication to this morning routine.
2. Learn to take full responsibility for everything that happens in your life, and trust that the universe is guiding you on a path that will help you be the most awakened person that you can become. Always ask, "What is the lesson here?"
3. Give yourself permission to realize that the journey to your heart may involve some painful encounters and may take a lifetime. Never give up. Find a therapist whom you connect with and who can help you overcome some past emotional traumas.
4. Begin a yoga practice. Find a certified yoga teacher who will teach you about the energy centers of your body and the mind-body connection. Since beginning a yoga practice, I have been

learning about this connection to pain and repressed emotions. I am finding my inner power and voice, which is helping me believe in myself and leading me to become the most authentic person that I can be.

5. There needs to be a harmonious relationship between work, rest, exercise, and play. Give yourself permission to have fun. Do things that you enjoyed as a child. Heal the inner child by learning to love yourself. Bring happiness to your heart. Begin a journey of self-love by being kind and compassionate to yourself. Build your emotional awareness by being present so that you can be aware of the lessons the universe continues to offer.

WHAT IS YOUR NEXT?

Realize that you are not alone on this journey. I continue this journey of awakening on a daily basis, and I try to stay awake to the lessons the universe presents to me. Some days, I have to admit I am snoozing. I encourage you to be open to the lessons the universe provides. But rest assured they will continue to repeat themselves until they are ready to be learned. If you are interested in reading more about my journey of awakening and how you or someone you know can begin to awaken a little more each day, check out my website at FromtheHeartwithMaggieSullivan.com.

ABOUT MAGGIE SULLIVAN

Maggie Sullivan is committed to her mission to provide information to people on how to obtain greater self-awareness and more inner peace. Over the past ten years, she has been working on waking herself up a little more each day. And her goal is to stay awake! Now, she is ready to help others wake up and reach their highest potential. Maggie is a trained educator who received her bachelor and master of arts in sociology and her bachelor of education. Over the past twenty years, she has been teaching in the elementary school system, and she is now planning to use her skills to guide people of all ages along their own journeys. She is a certified life coach and a Jack Canfield Success Principle trainer. She is the owner of From the Heart Wellness Centre, a center that provides a space for people to connect and receive services for their well-being. Maggie is currently blogging on her life lessons and is in the process of publishing her first book, *Life Lessons after I Woke Up*.

Chapter 20

MORE THAN A ZERO

When I was a child, my most treasured gifts were new journals. The feel of the blank pages, waiting for words, brought me indescribable joy. Find me near a stationery store, and I would disappear, running my fingers across the fresh paper, dreaming of the stories I could shape. Everywhere I went I felt inspired and dreamed of one day sharing my words with the world, writing books that would find themselves on best-seller lists and bedside tables across the continent.

I played with poetry and short stories, and when I entered high school, my talent was recognized by the head of the English department. A small creative writing class was established, and a group of four or five of us would gather on Friday afternoons in the meeting room off the library. There, tucked away from the busyness of the school, we would dive into stream-of-consciousness writing and writing exercises. In that quiet room, pen moving effortlessly across the paper, I felt as if I was truly showing up as I was meant to, congruent with my soul's purpose. The pain of my broken family and the depression and anxiety that had plagued me throughout my childhood were transformed into power as they shaped essays and stories, as my truths became words.

But the next year, everything changed.

I entered my eleventh-grade English class tentative but excited. I was fast-tracking, committed to my English studies and my dream of being a writer, so all the other students were a year older than I was. I settled in a desk in the middle of the room—not too close to but not too far from the teacher.

The other students filled in, most seeming not all that interested in being there, but when the bell rang, they settled in their seats. The teacher, a stern-faced woman, rose from her desk and started handing out the class outline, a document that had always excited me—a few simple pages stapled together, telling us of all we would explore and discover together over the coming months. I flipped through quickly, trying not to let the other students see my joy.

Clearing her throat, the teacher started to describe the primary assignment that would make up most of our grade that term. With each word she spoke, doubt and fear washed over me. What she was asking us to do I didn't understand at all—"symbolism," "foreshadowing," and "pathetic fallacy." These weren't terms I had worked with before, but everyone else seemed to know what was expected. I dared not admit that I did not. I was already pushing it to be in this class a year early; I was not about to prove to anyone that I wasn't supposed to be there by opening my mouth and admitting defeat on the very first day.

Over the next couple of months, I fumbled my way through that assignment. Finally, after many extensions, the teacher laid on my desk the result of my efforts. I looked down in horror. A large slash of thick red marker went from corner to corner across the page, topped off with a zero. A zero. A mark of 30 percent lay beneath the thick red marker, but owing to never meeting any of the deadline extensions, I had lost each one of those measly thirty marks.

Zero. Hot tears.

Zero. Total failure.

Zero. Dreams crushed.

I had never failed anything before, let alone received a zero. It was so definite, so absolute in its zeroness that I was convinced it spoke to my talent and potential, or lack thereof. To me, this one zero was everything, and my dream of being a writer became, in that moment, pointless, doomed for failure. I walked out of that classroom heartbroken, leaving my identity as a writer behind, discarded in the old wooden desks marked with years of students' disillusionment.

In the years that followed, convinced I didn't "get" literature, I chose the easiest English classes offered at my school, even going down a grade level, and at one point switched high schools as the rumor was the other school had a more lenient English department. Still, I carried my journal with me most places, and when I was without it, I wrote on whatever I could find.

One night, wandering the streets after dark with my friends, all of us up to no good, I came across a large piece of cardboard left beside a Dumpster behind an old restaurant. Inspiration hit, a Sharpie was provided, and a poem appeared on what was previously just a piece of recycling. My friends loved it, but truthfully, I disregarded this, convinced they loved it because they loved me. Even though the burst of creativity had fed my soul, nourished me in ways I knew I was meant to be fed, I considered it frivolous. Yet the cardboard poem lived on my bedroom wall for years, a constant reminder that the words were waiting and inspiration was everywhere.

But life went on. I entered university not knowing what to study; the only English course I dared to take counted also as a first-year women's studies credit, which was the only reason I took it. Once again we were reading old literature I felt had little to do with my own human experience, and I struggled to make sense of the ideas, to connect with the words. Conversely, in other classes I found myself ecstatic with the number of thought essays I had to write, shaping psychology, philosophy, and sociology concepts with ease. At one point I was convinced that my calling in life was writing university essays, and if my ethics hadn't gotten in the way, I'm sure I could have made a bundle as an essay writer for busy and disinterested students.

Instead I pursued psychology and received my designation as a registered professional counselor, committed to helping youth find peace and stability in their lives, something that I continued to find elusive. But still, all I really wanted to do was write. My favorite workdays as a youth addictions counselor were the ones that I got to head upstairs with a cup of tea in my hand and settle in the staff resource room in front of the computer to write my case reports.

From there I moved on to work as a youth and family counselor in the school board and explored numerous graduate options. Although I had loved school (all the essays!), I just couldn't commit to two more years of psychology or social-work education. Nothing excited me enough, and I often wondered where I would end up, whether I was destined to be an unsatisfied and burned-out front-line worker, dreams forgotten.

Then I got pregnant.

Twenty-eight years old, the man of my dreams, and a surprise pregnancy. Although we had been together only a year, we knew we were in it for the long haul and decided to go ahead and build a family. So there I was, looking at a few years of pregnancies, breastfeeding, and mat leaves as we hoped to have another child a couple of years after our first. Suddenly graduate school was off the table. Getting a job I enjoyed more than my current one seemed silly since there was no way I would have been able to start somewhere new and make as much as I was making. I felt stuck, as if my life had skidded to a halt. I realized that I was going to become a mother despite having no idea what I was going to do with my career. I was uninspired and out of time.

Staring down a hot and sticky, pregnant, and unemployed summer (one of the perks of working for the school board), with friends who would be scaling mountains while I tried to keep cool growing a baby, I jumped when an opportunity to attend a three-week career- and life-coaching program came my way. A good long look at my life—that's what I needed! Even though I couldn't make a move into a new job, maybe I could make a plan, perhaps even do some courses while on mat leave.

I drove an hour into the city each day, Monday to Friday, for three weeks to hang out in a nice air-conditioned room doing personality and skills assessments. I dug deep into my feelings about my career, sharing my dreams, hopes, and fears with the group of fifteen or so other adults in the search for something new. With each assessment I was brought back to writing. Test after test, it kept coming up.

Each time, my breath caught in my throat. Tears brimmed.

Writer.

There it was. Again. And again.

Writer.

And suddenly, with thirteen years of perspective and a baby growing inside me, I wondered whether maybe that zero had been wrong. Whether maybe that zero was just a zero and not my identity. Maybe it didn't actually say anything about who I was or who I could become.

At the end of the three-week program, each of us took turns standing at the front of the room to present our newly chosen career paths. When it was my turn, I heaved myself out of my chair, having already gained forty of the fifty extra pounds I carried in that pregnancy. I walked up to the front of the classroom and looked out over the table at these people who had been on this journey with me. With my hands on my growing belly and tears rimming my eyes, I told them that although I didn't really know where life was going to take me over the next few years, I could promise them one thing: "I will follow my dream of being a writer, one way or another. I have to because I am about to be the most important role model in this child's life. And if I'm going to tell him to follow his dreams no matter what anyone says, then I need to follow my own."

Between the birth of my first son and my second, I started exploring this new commitment. I took courses in marketing and public relations. I had a short writing contract for a green tech company, was a rep for a local family magazine, and on occasion did a few stints with the school board to keep some form of money coming in. Mostly, I mothered but did so knowing that my time would come again and I wouldn't play it safe. I would take the risk and write the words I knew my soul needed to write.

Three years after standing at the front of that room, I was crippled with postpartum depression following the birth of my second son, isolated in our little bit of suburbia and exhausted by my full-time job keeping the baby safe from his very jealous older brother. Stress, sadness, and disappointment filled every cell in my body. This was not the motherhood I had imagined. Each day felt like torture—a mix of toddler temper tantrums, endless breastfeeding, attempted napping, constant vigilance, and my own deep sadness weighing me down. I was consumed by grief, and the only thing that made me feel better was writing.

But this time, I didn't keep the words in a journal. I put them all online.

My openness and vulnerability were instantly appreciated. I started getting messages from mothers around the world who were reading my words late at night after the kids had gone to bed or hidden in the bathroom trying to get a few minutes' peace mid-day. Mothers who were sad and frustrated and convinced they were alone in their experience were finally reassured that there was another mother out there who shared their pain.

For me, on the keyboard side of the mommy blog, each post brought me into deeper alignment with my soul, and I could feel the realizing of my long-held but once-cast-aside dream. My words, the ones I had kept hidden from the public for years, were finally going out and having an impact, connecting with other women, showing them, and me, that the struggles we face are not ours alone.

I wrote my way through that depression and grew a business too. Women wanted to write as I did, open and free and honest. I coached them to tell their truths, taught them how to shape their wisdom into words. And suddenly, there I was, writing and teaching women how to write. It was far from a straight path, but somehow, with little boys at my feet looking up to me, I had landed myself right in the middle of my lifelong dream. Writing had seen me through the worst, stayed by my side at each turn, and finally, when I was ready, gifted me with the courage I needed to share my words with the world and inspire women to share theirs too.

ABOUT PARRISH WILSON

Parrish Wilson is a writing coach as well as a book editor for women who know they have words in their soul that need to find their way onto the page. It's her mission to create safe and accessible opportunities for women to pursue their dreams of writing and self-expression, whether the words live only in their journals or are destined to be published. She does this through online workshops and in-person retreats, creating beautiful and nurturing experiences designed to enhance the exploration of creativity with a spirit of playfulness and truth.

In between workshops, retreats, and parenting two young boys, Parrish tucks herself away in her office, immersed in the writing of her first full-length manuscript, due to be published in the summer of 2018. A memoir of her earliest years as a parent, struggling with postpartum depression and a high-needs child, Parrish's first book will be an intimate look at the truth of mental illness and how devastating it can be for new mothers and their families.

You can read more of Parrish's writing on mental health and motherhood here: www.patreon.com/parrishwilson

You can join Parrish in her free writing group on Facebook, Writing Vibes: www.facebook.com/groups/writingvibes

And you can find more goodies and free offerings from her here: www.parrishwilson.com/start-here/

Conclusion: Resource Platform

INSPIRED TO SHARE YOUR MESSAGE?

Heather DeSantis has joined us as a publicity resource, so that you can take the next steps in sharing your inspirational story!

Our hope is that you are not only inspired by this book but also have the tools and resources to bring your message out into the world. Here is a step-by-step strategy from our public relations expert.

YOUR MEDIA MESSAGE

Did you know that the media is looking for stories and experts just like you to share with their audience?

It's true!

Let me guess. Maybe deep down you have a greater story to share with the world—one that goes beyond money and success and gets down to the deeper purpose within you.

You might be a busy six- or seven-figure entrepreneur, and while you know that media is one way to really boost your credibility and make a bigger splash in the world, you have no idea how to get your voice heard in a sea of noise, but you're ready to stop playing small and start sharing your expertise.

Or maybe deep down you have a desire to share your obstacles and lessons with others, but the whole idea of getting press has you more than a little confused. Are you supposed to call radio stations? Send out a press release? The whole thing is kind of confusing; am I right?

You know that getting media coverage isn't just a good idea; it's necessary for your business if you want to become the go-to gal in your industry. But how do you get your story out there with all the noise in the marketplace?

Here's the thing: you can step into the spotlight and get seen as the expert you are; you just need someone to help you get there!

Lucky for you, this is where I shine.

I'm Heather DeSantis, and I'm a publicist and brand evangelist for heart-centered entrepreneurs who have a story that they simply must share with the world. I work with female entrepreneurs and lifestyle brands to help them get media coverage so that they can go on to do more greatness in the world!

My clients are in many industries, but what keeps them all connected is that their hearts and souls go into their businesses, and they have stories that help them connect with audiences and make a difference. I know that when you take a great story and add passion, plus massive action, it's a recipe for serious results!

You bring the story and passion, and I will bring the massive action to make sure you succeed. As someone with a lot of media relationships, I can tell you this: if you and I work together, you will see results.

I'm probably one of the only publicists who guarantee results, but I know that if you have a story that must be shared, paired with lots of heart, the media will adore you!

I believe that with the right press, you can take your business anywhere.

Results are my jam—nothing makes me more excited than securing an amazing press opportunity for my clients and watching them shine.

When you're growing your brand, you need a brand evangelist in your corner—rooting you on and helping to make sure you are the go-to industry leader the media wants to hear from!

How did I get here?

My career in PR began at a top PR agency working with entrepreneurs, health coaches, nutritionists, and even the NFL (seriously, how fun, right?). I was responsible for securing thirty-five placements per week for clients (yep, you read that right!). What I learned was that I thrive in a results-driven environment and that results are 100 percent attainable when you work hard.

My job at the PR firm was a dream job in some ways—I got to work with amazing clients, really honed my pitching skills, and learned a lot along the way. What was missing from my life was the ability to take time off when I wanted to, the flexibility to travel, and my desire to be more involved in philanthropy. In my heart and soul, I knew I was made to do much more, so I made a really big decision. I took a big leap and moved back home with my mom to pursue my true calling in life—to create a PR community to help my fellow female entrepreneurs—and that's when Boss Babe PR was born! I got a part-time job in the fitness industry (another big passion of mine) and set out to partner with my tribe and take them to the top! Now I get to work with amazing clients, helping them grow their businesses, and get paid in the process. Seriously, pinch me!

My expertise combined with my drive for results means that my clients enjoy guaranteed results. I am seriously so excited when it comes to getting press for my clients because I know the effect that well-placed press can have on your business (hint: it's huge!).

While my time at the PR firm helped me figure out that I wanted to have my own PR agency, my entrepreneurial spirit began at a much younger age.

My dad and my uncle were making it big in real estate, and they were the first to introduce me to the world of business ownership. I loved seeing the dedication they both had to their work and the drive that ultimately led to their mega success. I knew it was something I was destined to have in life. Another thing that I attribute to my success is the fact that I was adopted when I was three days old. I really believe that my parents created in me a desire to be part of something greater than myself through their demonstration of love for me.

I've always been someone with a drive to work hard and go after my dreams. For instance, when I was in college, I worked with at-risk teen girls and helped them have better futures. I also persuaded the CEO of Livestrong to speak at my college graduation (how's that for persistence?).

I began my first LLC, called Romp Away, in 2012, and while it was super fun (I bought clothes from a local thrift store and upcycled them into rompers and headbands—so cute!), I realized it wasn't going to be profitable, but at this point I was completely sold on being my own boss. I ended up getting involved with network marketing through Beachbody, a decision that solidified my love for the health and wellness industries. I am currently attending the Institute of Integrative Nutrition, and I adore working with health coaches, nutritionists, personal trainers, and others in the health and wellness fields (something that my three years as a food publicist uniquely positioned me for!).

In 2016, I began my own PR agency and started working with dream clients (like you!) to help them get their stories out and make a difference in their industries.

Working with heart-centered entrepreneurs and securing press for my clients is something that I am super passionate about!

SO JUST WHAT IS PR?

You might be asking, just what exactly is public relations (street name: PR)?

PR is the act of getting media attention to your business by getting you featured on local news, in national media, on podcasts, on the radio, and in print newspapers. There's a lot that goes into PR, and when you choose to work with me, you can focus on your story and leave the pitching to me!

When it comes to PR, I like to think of myself as more than just someone pitching your brand to the media. I'm your ambassador and your brand evangelist! Seriously, I'll sing your praises from every rooftop and make sure the media knows not only that you exist but also that you are the best person to tell the story that only you can tell.

When you work with me, I can do it all: from writing the pitch content, to contacting the media, to following up. It's full-service PR with a very personalized approach. My packages range from 100 percent done-for-you PR services to a monthly subscription where I coach you on how to get media placements for yourself. My passion is broadcast media, TV, and radio, owing to the emotions and physical touch that viewers can get from seeing you, but I love national media too.

I seriously love PR because it's one of the fastest ways to grow your business in today's content-rich world. With so many people angling to be heard in the world of advertising, getting press for your business means you will get a featured spot on a news show or radio program so you can begin connecting with your perfect-match audiences.

TIPS TO FOLLOW TO GET ON TV

As entrepreneurs we are always looking for creative ways to grow our businesses to gain more raving fans and create more clients or consumers. In this day and age, most businesses are building their empires online because it feels natural. We live in a virtual world, and it gives us instant feedback. An online business is also portable and allows flexibility to choose when and where we work. But what if we want to build a business that has a stronger presence?

Are you tired of building a business only behind a computer screen? Do you feel it is time to create brand recognition much greater than Facebook? Would you like your business to be better known locally, regionally, or nationally? What if you would *love* to be on TV but have no media contacts or do not know where to start?

What if you wanted to share your message with millions? Securing yourself TV and radio segments will increase your influence and credibility, position you as an expert, and allow you to share your message with people at a much faster rate.

1. Research your local market.

First and foremost, prosper where your feet are, and focus on your hometown! Stations *love* local on-air talent. Once you have experience promoting your business services or products, consider targeting new cities or even cities you will be traveling to that year. Spend time watching local TV morning shows and listening to radio stations to see what types of interviews and guests they prefer. Spend time finding the media personalities on social media, and connect with them. Establish the message and mission you want to share.

2. Establish your story and pitch.

Once the product or service is identified, brainstorm key elements and benefits you feel comfortable discussing—for example, how to become organized, tips for healthy eating, key things to look for when buying a new house, and so on.

Tip: Combining your expertise with an upcoming national awareness day (Mother's Day, American Heart Month, etc.) may help your promotion effort. Or current national or regional news may create a need for broadcasters to find experts like you to provide more detailed information. After you know your key topics and the product or service you will promote, you are ready to pitch the media!

Be confident!

3. Write and e-mail your pitch.

First make a list of all TV and radio stations in your target market. Gather the producers' e-mail addresses simply by going to the stations' websites or calling the stations to get the best e-mail addresses to send a pitch to.

Producers work early in the morning, so consider contacting them before ten o'clock.

Send the producer a *short* e-mail introducing yourself.

Ask to be a guest on his or her morning show.

Summarize the concept of your talk and include three or four bullet points.

4. Follow up.

When you connect with the media, be sure you listen more than you speak and ask the producer directly whether he or she has on-air guests.

If the producer says yes, briefly ask him or her whether you can be a guest on the show, and share three to four topics that you can discuss.

Send a follow-up e-mail to the producer twenty-four hours after your initial e-mail.

Call the station, and ask to speak to the producer within forty-eight to seventy-two hours.

Introduce yourself and assume the producer did not receive your e-mail and ask to be a guest on his or her morning show.

5. Promote on social media.

Before the Interview

• Post on social media and tag the station, sharing your excitement to be on the station.

• Share with your e-mail list that you are going to be interviewed, and share with your community how they can check out the interview.

• Three days prior, promote the segment across all your social-media channels, tagging the stations and highlighting the key things you will be sharing.

• Promote your interview in your Facebook group.

• Consider how you want to capture leads! Create a lead page and promote a freebie or your free Facebook community.

Day of Media

• If you are doing a studio segment, check in on social media! If you are doing a phone interview, take a selfie and post on social media.

• Ask the anchors to take a photo with you!

• Have a friend do a Facebook Live of you at the segment getting interviewed.

After the Interview

- After the segment, work with Heather DeSantis PR to get the TV or radio clip.
- Post the raw interview footage on your business Facebook page, and boost the interview.
  - TV clips can be bought from a third-party clipping service.
- Share the interview with your e-mail list.
- Upload the interview onto your website.
- Ensure all media are added to the media page on your website.
- Update your bio to include media that have interviewed you.
- Update your profile picture to be a photo of you on TV!
- Send a link of your recent media appearances to potential clients.
- Leverage media logos.

The most important thing to remember is the world needs what you have to offer! I can't wait to see your message soon!

I'm passionate about getting press coverage for food brands, charities, and entrepreneurs. I've been a publicist for five years and each week secure thirty-plus new media opportunities for my clients. By working together, we will increase your influence, credibility, and following, which will position you as an internationally known leader.

Our mission is to focus on publicity with a purpose: your purpose! Do you want to grow your brand through television exposure? Are you seeking to position yourself as an expert in your field through interviews and media spotlights? Would you like to promote a book or charitable cause? We will provide you the publicity to fulfill your purpose.

Heather DeSantis of Heather DeSantis Public Relations—The Influencer Revolution

http://www.desantispr.com/

heather@desantispr.com

ABOUT THE CREATOR OF
THE *INSPIRED IMPACT BOOK*
SERIES AND MOVEMENT

Here I was, a stay-at-home-mompreneur with two gorgeous little girls, a supportive hubby and a semi-fancy house, I thought I had it made! Until that sneaky little thing called 'life purpose' began gnawing at my soul.

You see, at 27-years-old when I was diagnosed with a fatal heart condition, I had made a deal with God. I vowed to God that if I could be given the opportunity of more time, that I would vow to always show up for my life.

He did, and so did I… or so I thought.

I showed up in my role as a mom, a wife, and a mom-preneur, believing I was keeping up my end of the deal. But there was one problem, no where in my life was I truly showing up for myself. I did not realize it at first. I mean, c'mon...I was busy and I mean, *super* busy. I was doing *all the things.*

You know how it is, right? Waking up to hit the ground running, dashing off to this and that and a calendar so jam packed you can't find time to schedule your doctor appointments, return your best friend's call or get out for a date night. I mean, date night?! What's that again?

When I realized this, my world turned upside down. This was not just a journey to slow down or find my passion...no! I had made a deal with God! I had vowed to always show up for my life, and that meant showing up for me.

One day the pull got so strong, I had no choice but to surrender. And what I thought would be the scariest journey of my life, because it was unknown, ended up being a path of miracles... everywhere.

This journey started for me in 2012. Now, just five years later I am a #1 best-selling author, working on publishing my 7th bestseller, a Certified Professional Success Coach and an expert with the Law of Reciprocity.

Through my journey of self-discovery and working with incredible mentors (one of which wrote the Foreword in this book), I was able to gain clarity on my soul's highest path. My core genius is helping women gain clarity on *their* life purpose to create visions and goals that align with their highest path and then create applicable actions to bring it to life.

My philosophies are to love more, give more and care more than necessary...always. Not because it will come back to you (although it will), but because it's what I believe is right.

I'm here to serve others, sprinkle glitter, spread magic, make a massive impact on the world and help all my clients do the same.

I am the coach that will meet you where you are, without judgment or confinement. My expertise lies in coaching women through transition, transformation and up-levels in life.

There was a time in my life when I was just going through the motions, but I could feel in my gut there was more for me. Patty Aubery showed me it was possible, and she changed my stars. And now it's my life's mission to help you change yours.

With a
Grateful Heart
— Kate ♡

Kate Butler is a #1 Best Selling Author, Certified Professional Success Coach and International Speaker. Kate has been featured on HBO, in the Huffington Post and many other news and radio platforms.

Kate had the honor of being featured in Jack Canfield's newest release, *Living the Success Principles* and also sharing the speaking stage with him. She has also shared the keynote stage with celebrity cooking sensation, Laura Vitale and forward thought leader, Marianne Williamson.

Kate's children's books have received the prestigious Mom's Choice Award for Excellence®, the Readers Favorite International Book Award® and have also been endorsed by popular children's brands, Kidorable® and the Garden State Discovery Museum™.

Kate received her degree in Mass Communication and Interpersonal Communication Studies from Towson University,

MD. After 10 years in the corporate industry, Kate decided it was time to go into business for herself.

Kate's passion is intuitively coaching her clients through their own transformations and breakthroughs so they can identify their life's mission and begin living on their highest path. Kate accomplishes this through her books, 1:1 & group coaching work and live events. Her mission is to guide people to step into their light and ignite their life

Ways to work with Kate:

Coaching - You're invited to experience more miracles in your life through the Pathway to Miracles coaching program. In this program, Kate coaches you through the 37 most common ways we block miracles in our personal, professional and daily lives and how you can stop blocking them so you can unlock the pathway to miracles and live your greatest life. Kate takes a practical approach on how you can create real miracles in your everyday life and in this program, miracles are guaranteed.

Visit: www.katebutlercoaching.com/miracles

Publish a book - You're invited to become a part of the next book in the Inspired Impact Series! *Women Who Ignite* was our first #1 best-selling book in the series. The success of that book brought us to create this 2nd book, *Women Who Inspire*. The next book in the series is *Women Who Influence*, followed by *Women Who Impact*. If you have always dreamed of sharing your story or publishing a book, then this may be for you!

Visit: www.katebutlercoaching.com/books

Speaking - Whether you are hosting an intimate women's circle or a massive seminar, Kate would love to support your work by speaking at your next event. Kate is not just an inspirational speaker, but also an ***experiential*** speaker, bringing the audience through exercises that will create energy shifts and mindset expansion right there on the spot. The audience will leave feeling inspired, empowered, uplifted and with a renewed sense of clarity. Kate's main mission is to inspire women to align with their soul's path and she would love to partner with you in order to impact more people!

To connect for collaboration: www.katebutlercoaching.com/speaking

Are you a Woman Who Ignites?
Are you a Woman Who Inspires?
Are you a Woman Who Influences?
Are you a Woman Who Impacts?

Then we want to connect with *you*!
The Inspired Impact Movement is looking to connect with women who desire to share their story and serve the world. If you have dreamed of publishing a book, then this is for you. If you have dreamed of bringing your message to a larger audience, then this is for you. If you have dreamed of exposing your business through a new platform, then this is for you. If you have dreamed of inspiring women all over the globe, then this is for you.
We want to hear your story!

Visit: www.katebutlercoaching.com/influence

May your soul be so inspired, that you are moved to inspire others.

Wishing you divine clarity, abundance, miracles, and a swirl of inspiration along your journey!

With love and gratitude,

the women who inspire

PERMISSIONS

Mary Anne Munning. Reprinted with permission.
Desiree Peterkin Bell. Reprinted with permission.
Melissa Binkley. Reprinted with permission.
Shawn Ciociola. Reprinted with permission.
Aubree Deimler. Reprinted with permission.
Jenna Edwards. Reprinted with permission.
Jenny Fenig. Reprinted with permission.
Lauren Fisher. Reprinted with permission.
Kimberly Flatland. Reprinted with permission.
Missy A. Garcia. Reprinted with permission.
Tally Hayden. Reprinted with permission.
Jen Heilman. Reprinted with permission.
Lea Imsiragic. Reprinted with permission.
Lisa Khera. Reprinted with permission.
Pamela Michelle. Reprinted with permission.
Brooke Rash. Reprinted with permission.
Mandy Scanlon. Reprinted with permission.
Jewell Siebert. Reprinted with permission.
Maggie Sullivan. Reprinted with permission.
Parrish Wilson. Reprinted with permission.
Heather DeSantis. Reprinted with permission.